INSIDE THE GAME

PAULINE CARTWRIGHT

Published by Pearson Education Limited, Edinburgh Gate, Harlow, Essex, CM20 2JE
Registered company number: 872828

www.pearsonschools.co.uk

First published by Pearson Education New Zealand
a division of Pearson New Zealand Ltd
67 Apollo Drive, Rosedale, North Shore 0632, New Zealand
Associated companies throughout the world

Text © Pauline Cartwright 2009

Page Layout and Design: Ruby-Anne Fenning
Chapter Illustrations: Fisheye Design, Sydney, Australia

The right of Pauline Cartwright to be identified as author of this work has been
asserted by her in accordance with the Copyright, Designs and Patents Act 1988.

First published 2009
This edition published 2012

22
10

British Library Cataloguing in Publication Data
A catalogue record for this book is available from the British Library

ISBN 978-0-43507-611-5

Printed and bound in Great Britain by Bell and Bain Ltd, Glasgow

Acknowledgements
We would like to thank the children and teachers of Bangor Central Integrated
Primary School, NI; Bishop Henderson C of E Primary School, Somerset; Brookside
Community Primary School, Somerset; Cheddington Combined School,
Buckinghamshire; Cofton Primary School, Birmingham; Dair House Independent
School, Buckinghamshire; Deal Parochial School, Kent; Lawthorn Primary School,
North Ayrshire; Newbold Riverside Primary School, Rugby and Windmill Primary
School, Oxford for their invaluable help in the development and trialling of the Bug
Club resources.

Every effort has been made to contact copyright holders of material reproduced in
this book. Any omissions will be rectified in subsequent printings if notice is given
to the publishers.

A division of Pearson New Zealand Ltd

CONTENTS

It felt unbelievable – terrifying. Here he was, racing over a drawbridge, suspended over deep, black water. Real water! And he was expected to save a real person from real enemies! How could it be that he was inside the computer game?

But he was. Everything around him leapt out as real. Nothing was small, flat and non-dimensional, as it had been on the screen; it was all fully three-dimensional. And he was in it, part of it, shocked by its sudden, life-sized reality.

As he ran by them, each link of the chains strung along the drawbridge looked heavy and strong. He could even see small lumps of dirt that had built up on the outer curves of the links. The boards beneath his feet rattled and shook. Moss grew on their furthest edges, where no feet had reached to wear it off. In the dark water beneath him, a circle formed and rippled outwards from where a guard had thrown or dropped something in. Beside him, the astoundingly tiny princess was running, clutching her free hand to her crown, fleet-footed in her fear.

He was inside a computer game that just seconds ago he had been controlling from a seat in front of a screen. It had seemed such an ordinary thing to be doing, on an ordinary day . . .

Computers! A roomful of computers of so many different models and ages. Chris couldn't believe how it had changed since the only other time he had been here. He felt a rush of excitement and an answering twitch in his fingers. Which of these was Uncle Reg's oldest computer? If it was here, would it still have the *Seven Missions* game on it?

Of course there was the strong possibility that Uncle Reg might have got rid of an old computer and an old game like that years ago. Then again, it could be that Uncle Reg had been keeping his old models, creating a kind of museum of computers, saving the early programmes and games. Chris really hoped so. *Seven Missions* was the first computer game he had ever played – the one that had hooked him. It was the one that had convinced him that computers were more than simply useful and sometimes interesting.

Chris thought of it now as his introduction into the computer world, a world where, he believed, he would eventually choose a career.

His parents had watched his growing attachment to computers and called it an addiction; they'd insisted he gave time to other interests as well. At first he'd felt resentful but he admitted now that he was glad he had been pushed into outside interests. He'd become a crack swimmer, cleaning up the prizes at the last school swimming sports. He'd found snorkelling a blast and wanted to do more of that – maybe learn to scuba-dive one day.

Most of all, he loved rock climbing. Sometimes he grinned to himself when he thought that his parents' introduction had led to yet another addiction.

His cousin Amy was pretty keen on rock climbing, too, and they'd shared the hobby together. Over the years, Amy had spent a lot of holiday time, and sometimes weekends, at Chris's home. Her mother often had to go away on business and both sets of parents liked to think that, because Amy and Chris were both only children, time spent with each other would create a family-sibling feeling between them. Chris actually *did* think of Amy as a sister.

Chris swivelled around slowly, savouring the pleasure this room gave him. He knew Amy didn't feel the same way about computers. She hardly ever asked him for a turn on his computer, unless she had a school project to work on. But to him this roomful of machines was bliss.

"Isn't this something!" he hissed at his cousin.

"Sure is – for a computer geek."

Chris wanted her to share the excitement that fizzed inside him, not dampen it with her own lack of enthusiasm. And he disliked being called a geek.

"Well," he said, a little sulkily, "you're a book freak."

Amy shrugged, not at all offended. "I just like books better. Computers are useful but I don't want to spend my spare time staring at a screen. I'd rather turn pages."

Chris moved away from her towards the hessian-covered screen that divided the large basement room into two sections. He could hear his Auntie May and his mother still talking in the doorway so he called out, "What's behind here?"

Auntie May called back, "That's the time travel section."

Chris felt the hairs rise on the back of his neck. "Time travel?"

But Auntie May didn't respond to his excitement. She had turned back to her sister, Chris's mother, and he could hear her saying, "You know me and computers. We've never had more than a nodding acquaintance. For Reg, computers were his life, along with all the technology linked to them. I think he thought anything on this earth could be made possible with the aid of computers. Anything."

May was a successful artist who had always seemed completely absorbed in her painting and sculpting. But Chris still felt a faint sense of surprise that she'd never wanted to investigate computers, if only for the graphic programmes on them.

His aunt was walking over to him and Amy now. "As I said when we came down, it'll be just fine if you two want to amuse yourselves with a game. I know there are some on these computers and you'll know how to find them. Your mum tells me you know all about computers, Chris. But that gear you're looking at now might best be left alone."

Chris and Amy were peering at the electronic equipment behind the hessian screen. There were curious items sitting on the floor and others on a long bench. From some of them, linking cables ran through holes in the screen to computers on the other side. Chris felt ripples of excitement running over him just looking at it. What did it all do?

Amy had picked up a headset that included an optical visor and was turning it over in her hands. It was most likely associated with some sort of virtual reality equipment, thought Chris, before going back to his aunt's earlier comment. "Did you say this was the time travel section?"

Auntie May laughed. "Well, that's what I called it – just for fun really. Reg was always experimenting, trying to invent things, and he did talk sometimes about time travel. I think he just loved dreaming about the possibility of it. So that's how I came to call this tangle of technology the time travel section. Actually though, I think it had more to do with virtual reality, plus the work he was doing on computer games for the software company."

Her face fell a little. "I've put off Reg's friends who wanted to help me sort out all the stuff in this room. But I think it's about time now to deal with it."

Chris's mother put an arm around May's shoulder and they began to murmur together in low voices. It was why Chris's mother had been driving the relatively long distance to visit more frequently than usual. Her sister was still finding it difficult to cope with her husband's death.

Chris had been shocked when he heard Uncle Reg had died. He hadn't thought of him as old. As they were driving over he had tried to imagine how his aunt must feel, knowing her husband – dead now for six months – would never be coming back. Never was a long time…

The little Chris remembered of his only lengthy visit to his aunt and uncle, when he was eight, was good. He could recall Reg's warm chuckle when Chris had discovered the excitement of playing *Seven Missions* on the old computer while Uncle Reg did something that looked much less interesting on a small laptop. Chris had appreciated that Reg made no attempt to encourage him to do something else, as his mother would have done.

He remembered that Uncle Reg had owned three computers then, and he'd found that amazing. Now there was a roomful of them and all this electronic gear as well! Chris wished suddenly that Uncle Reg were alive to explain all the details to him.

"The games will be on the computers over the other side of the room," continued Auntie May. "You can't do any harm looking for a game or two, so choose yourselves a computer, switch it on – you might have to plug it in first – and check there's a game there. We'll leave you to it."

"What's the game you want?" asked Amy when the sisters had wandered out of the basement, still deep in conversation. "Something about missions, wasn't it?"

Chris figured she was making an effort to be interested and appreciated it. "It's called *Seven Missions*. I don't know if you'll like it or not. It's not one of the modern games. It mightn't even be here any more."

"Who knows? I might like an old-fashioned one better than some of the other ones I've seen, so go for it. Choose what you like. You know more than I do about all this."

Amy trailed behind Chris as he left the mysterious machines behind the hessian screen and made his way around the computers on the other side of the room.

"Look!" he cried, stopping in front of a squat, square box, his hands stretched out as if to hug it. "Look at this! I reckon this is the computer I used with Uncle Reg when I was eight."

"It certainly looks ancient," said Amy, laughing.

"It wasn't *that* long ago!" protested Chris. "But I guess it was a pretty old model even then, so I suppose it could be called ancient now. Let's try it out and see if it's still going."

The screen was rather small compared to some of the larger ones in the room and it took a few moments to come to life. Chris tapped a few keys, used the mouse to skim through a selection of files, tapped a few more keys and suddenly hissed with suppressed excitement. "It's here! Look at this."

Over his shoulder, Amy read:

CAN YOU GET THE LITTLE PRINCESS
SAFELY BACK TO HER KINGDOM?
SEVEN MISSIONS
LIE AHEAD!

Chris wriggled into a more comfortable position in front of the screen. The game was ready and waiting for him. How fantastic that Uncle Reg hadn't thrown it out. "This time I want to get to the end. The day I found this game, I played it over and over and I could *not* pass the Mountain Beast."

Amy wrinkled her nose. "The Mountain Beast? What's that?"

"You'll see. Maybe you can help me figure out how to get past it and keep the Little Princess safe."

"The Little Princess?" A hint of sarcasm had entered Amy's voice now.

"Like I said, it's an old game. But it's really cool. Honest. The princess has to be rescued and returned to her kingdom." Chris dragged a second chair over in front of the computer. "Sit down and I'll show you."

THE GUARDS WERE REAL

It was Chris who sat directly in front of the screen, Chris who controlled the mouse and the keyboard and chose the human icon to be "them" on-screen as they set out to meet the challenges of the game. But Amy – though not normally a computer game player – was quick with responses and suggestions.

"That was the easiest mission," said Chris when, in no time at all, they had accomplished the First Mission by searching the Darkest Jungle for the hidden jewel belonging to the Little Princess. "It keeps getting harder – and scarier."

The fiercest creature they'd had to contend with in the jungle search was a snarling panther. Amy had laughed at it and called it a "darling pussy cat" because it hadn't been difficult to chase away. After avoiding spiders and falling tree limbs in a wild storm and then coming to several dead ends on jungle pathways, they had finally found the jewel in a boat sunk deep in the river.

"That would have been the last place I'd have thought of looking," exclaimed Amy, as Chris revealed the remembered hiding place and an enlarged image of the precious stone glowed for a moment on the screen. "What's it for anyway? Why's the jewel so important?"

"The Little Princess can make lightning flash by throwing it into the air three times. No one else can do that. That's how the people in her kingdom know she's their princess – if she's carrying it and then proves her ownership by using it to create lightning."

"I still don't really get it. What's the point of making lightning?"

"Like I said, the fact that she knows how to use the jewel to make it proves she's the real princess and not an impostor." Chris was impatient to accomplish the Second Mission. "Being in control of lightning can be useful actually. You'll find that out!"

Back in the game, they were travelling through mountains where taking a wrong turn meant facing confrontations with bandits, and there were avalanches in the mountain passes.

"Quick! The other way!" shrieked Amy, drawn in by the excitement of the game. She seemed to have a second sense about avalanches poised to cut off their path. Three times they avoided a deluge of rocks and earth, and Chris's mouse finger was soon slick with sweat.

"That was quick! Second Mission over!" enthused Chris as they reached the other side of the Towering Mountains. He was thrilled to be rediscovering the magic he'd found in this game years ago. "This is a kid's game really and modern games are way more sophisticated, but I still reckon it's cool. Don't you?"

"It's not bad," allowed Amy. "I have to say I'm glad it's not all about killing people all the time. I think those games are gross."

Chris glanced at her. "We have to kill some animals later." He knew she was crazy about animals.

"Kill animals?" Amy frowned.

"Not cute cats and dogs and stuff – fantasy kinds of creatures that aren't one bit nice."

"Doesn't sound like my kind of thing."

Chris thought it wise to change the subject and turned back to the screen. "Anyway, now we cross the desert. Each mission gets a bit longer and a bit more complicated and our main thing in this one is finding water to survive. Actually, I've forgotten most of what worked best here."

"We'll need shelter, too," said Amy, pointing to a

blazing graphic sun that threatened to shrivel any living thing.

Chris would have skipped this mission if he could have. He didn't find it as exciting as the others, which was possibly why he hadn't retained a strong memory of the strategies required. But Amy seemed to be enjoying the problem-solving and quickly worked out that they should head into the valleys each time they ran out of water. They would find deep wells there if they searched carefully. She also discovered that carrying palm branches was one of the best ways to protect themselves from the sun on the long journeys between valleys.

Chris let her take a turn with the mouse and she developed an impressive skill for avoiding poisonous scorpions. In fact, she got so engrossed in the various challenges that she didn't seem to mind how long it took them to cross the sandy expanse.

Chris was much happier when they had finished that mission and begun the more thrilling Fourth Mission, in which they had to cross a landscape infested with giants and snakes, where the weather patterns were constantly changing.

It wasn't long before Amy began to lose interest though. "It doesn't seem right to kill all the snakes," she protested.

Chris made a face. "It's either them or us!"

They found their way over flooded rivers, by-passed a landslide and traversed a mountain in a snowstorm, successfully dealing with the dangerous inhabitants.

It was time for the Fifth Mission. Chris felt his excitement building. This time they would have to battle the enemies of the Little Princess directly, and snatch her from a castle prison. Banded together as an army, the enemies were an odd mix of dwarfs, giants, a monster or two and several soldiers bearing old-fashioned weapons. It was these last that seemed the most dangerous.

Amy got up from her chair. "I get sick of all this sort of stuff. Fighting, fighting . . . I'll come back later if you can convince me it's got a bit more interesting than it is now."

It was the wild action of the Fifth Mission that Chris loved most. He was so busy watching his back and slashing with his sword that he took no notice when Amy drifted away across the basement room.

His pulse raced as he found himself suddenly surrounded by enemies. For a moment he wondered whether he'd be able to escape at all, but he'd soon spotted a clear space to make for.

Eureka! He felled one soldier with a cunning

keystroke and, with a click of the mouse, leapt beyond the evil dwarfs clamouring for his blood. He was free! He had beaten the enemies and still held the jewel safely in one hand. His heart thumped as if he had actually been running a hard race.

Now he had to get into the enemy castle where the Little Princess was held. Chris knew it would be difficult – not quite as difficult as the Seventh Mission, the last one, but still very tricky. He didn't want to fail now and have to begin the entire game again, so he rested for a while, letting the game remain static on the screen. He glanced around the room. "Where are you, Amy?"

There was a bulging bookcase on one wall of the basement and Chris felt slightly surprised that Amy, the book lover, wasn't investigating it. His eyes wandered across the titles until his attention was caught and held by the names on two of the book spines: Stephen Hawking and H G Wells. Immediately, Chris's mind zinged back to his aunt's mention of time travel. Was it possible that Uncle Reg had filled a bookcase with books about the idea of time travel?

Suddenly, Amy's voice broke into his thoughts. "I'm over here," she called from behind the hessian room divider.

Chris cast about for a way to tempt her back to the game. "I'll be rescuing the princess in a minute. Then I'll need you to help me get past the Mountain Beast."

"Be there in a minute," called Amy. "You know, there's a strange-looking machine back here that has a cable going through the screen. I think it's joined up to the computer you're on now."

"Uh-huh," muttered Chris, not really listening. He'd begun playing again – creeping to the dungeon door at the foot of the castle. Every time the guard on the ramparts above looked down, he paused, because he remembered that stillness camouflaged him. Closer, closer. Now he was at the door. Now he was breaking it down, bashing at it with an iron crowbar propped nearby.

Then there she was – the Little Princess – small, like a very beautiful doll. He grabbed her hand and they ran over the splintered door and out of the dungeon. They were going to make it!

Above him, the guards were leaning and calling, their voices loud with anger. Chris hesitated for a second. He had never heard the guards *calling* before. He had *seen* them on the screen, moving and raging. But they didn't call out. This was an old game with limited sound effects and individual voices weren't among them. Yet it wasn't his imagination working overtime. *The guards were calling out!*

"There they are!"

"He broke open the dungeon door!"

"He has her – the Little Princess!"

"We mustn't let her get away!"

The voices were frightening to his ears – frighteningly *real*.

An eerie feeling made Chris look upwards. And there above him, life-sized, were the guards. *They were real!*

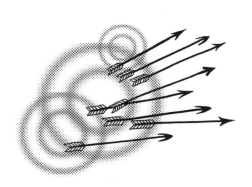

In front of him was a castle wall, each of its individual stones standing out, huge and rough. They were cold when he reached out a hand and touched them. *The wall was real!* A staircase wound down from the ramparts and the guards were using it to run towards him. What on earth was happening in his head? Why did he think the guards and the castle were real? It wasn't possible.

Chris shook his head and glanced down at his right hand. There was no computer mouse in it. There was only the hand of the Little Princess, and she, too, was real. Not a figure on a screen but a living, breathing girl – tiny and beautiful, a real golden crown glistening on her head. How could this be?

Chris's heart was thudding as he dropped the tiny hand and stared about him, trying to control the panic rising inside him. A mossy, damp smell rose from the stones of the castle. Once more he scanned the staircase winding up the wall, the battered and broken dungeon door and the dimness beyond. He saw the flash of silver swords approaching; he heard the rough, threatening cries of the guards.

The tiny hand of the Little Princess had taken hold of his arm now, her voice rising above the hubbub of clanking weapons, pounding feet and men's cries. "Quickly!" she prompted. "The guards are coming."

Chris had never heard her voice before. There was something about it that suggested a talking doll or some sort of digital toy. Yet it was clear and her eyes were clear, too – as clear as green glass. He was staring into a living, pleading face. He could do nothing but answer that plea.

"I'll save you!" cried Chris.

They were the words he had cried in his head when he had played this game before. But it wasn't happening on a screen any longer. He was in it, and it was terrifying! Here he was, racing over a drawbridge, suspended over real water that was deep and black. He was expected to save a real person from real enemies! How could it be that he was inside the game? But he was.

As he ran by them, each link of the chains strung along the drawbridge looked heavy and strong. The boards beneath his feet rattled and shook. Beside him, the tiny princess was also running, clutching her free hand to her crown, fleet-footed in her fear.

Chris realised that he was holding something in his left hand – something hard that felt slightly warm, as though it had been there for a while. Looking down, he glimpsed the glow of rainbow colours through his fingers and could not believe what he was holding. On the other side of the bridge, he let go of the princess and thrust out his hand – the jewel he and Amy had found in the First Mission was sparkling on his palm. With a cry of delight, the Little Princess snatched it away.

Chris's mind raced as he reviewed the moves he had made when he played the computer game on-screen. What he did then he must do again now – for real.

Stepping forward, he seized an axe leaning against a stone. It was heavy and the metal head was bound to the handle with what looked like a strip of leather. He raised it high above his head and brought it down wildly, over and over again, on the thick ropes that secured the drawbridge over the castle moat.

When the first rope separated, one end of it flew dramatically up into the air and the drawbridge tipped suddenly. Chris heard a protesting howl from a guard. He wished that he'd dared to wait until some of the pursuers were actually on the bridge. It would have been a sweet revenge, after the Little Princess's imprisonment, for her to see some of her jailers floundering in the moat.

The second rope was severed now and the guards, who had almost reached the other end of the drawbridge, leapt back as it swung down to smash against the wall of the moat. Howling angrily, other guards halted on the winding stairs and lifted their longbows, sending a shower of arrows raining down on Chris and the Little Princess as they turned and fled.

Running, running, running for their lives. It was easy enough to escape a rain of screen arrows using a mouse and computer keys, but the whistle of real arrows cutting the air was terrifying. As was the realisation of what would happen if one reached its target.

Now as they ran, a different voice called after

them. "Wait for me! *Wait!*"

Chris cast a fearful glance over his shoulder and realised with a lurch of his heart that the voice didn't belong to anyone he should fear. It was Amy – calling as she ran behind them.

"Where are we? What's happening?" She was panting as she caught up with them on the leaf-strewn roadway. A strange sound, somewhere between a hiss and a crack, sent her leaping off the road. "What's that?" she gasped, as an arrow sliced through the air close behind her.

Reason told Chris that it would be okay to slow his pace to a jog. The destruction of the drawbridge had cut off any possibility of the guards catching up with them. Though they had done their best with their longbows, they were too far back now for any arrows to reach their target. "It was an arrow," he told Amy. "But they're falling short. You'll be okay."

"An arrow!" Appalled, Amy peered fearfully behind her. She turned back to Chris and repeated, "Where are we? What's happening?" Then, her face turning into a mask of disbelief, she added, "*Who's that?*"

"I rescued her. She's the Little Princess," panted Chris. "I don't know how, but we're *in* the game. One minute I was playing it and now we're inside it! I can't understand it but we're part of it. What do *you* think happened?"

Though his head whirled with confusion, Chris also felt a rush of excitement sweep through him. The guards couldn't get them now that the drawbridge was down. He was winning! He was strong and powerful! He had rescued the Little Princess and he would save her! Energy surged into his running feet. He could run forever if he needed to.

The Little Princess tugged at his hand as she stumbled over something in the roadway and Chris slowed down a little.

Amy slowed, too, as she tried to make sense of what she had heard. "We can't be inside a computer game. It's not . . . It can't be possible to . . ." Amy's mind was racing, looking for connections. "Could it be a sort of illusion to do with that machine I fiddled with?"

Chris stopped running altogether now. "What do you mean?" he asked.

"Behind that screen. I was standing where one of the cords went through a hole and joined up with the computer we were playing on. I sort of wiggled it a bit to try and find out what it was joined on to and the other machine's lights went on."

"Lights?" Chris was staring at her.

"I ran back over to find you, and you weren't there. The computer screen was sort of still and blank so I moved the mouse to see if the game was still on or not and then . . ."

"And then?"

"And then I was *here*, with you. And with her." She pointed as the look of disbelief intensified on her face. "The Little Princess."

Chris could see how she would be astonished by the princess – by her tiny size, her beauty and her glistening crown. He was astonished himself. Someone who had been on the screen was now suddenly alive beside him. And the sight of her – right here in flesh and blood – made Chris want to save her more than when she had been a princess on the computer.

That would mean somehow getting her past the Mountain Beast waiting ahead of them. He had never been able to do that on the screen. How was he going to do it now, inside the game? It was an agony even to consider facing such a creature – with its terrible limbs and hideous face – actually alive. Instead, he forced his mind back to the puzzle of their situation.

"Sit down a minute." He gestured at the bank. "We're not in danger right here."

He peeled off his light, zipped jacket and, feeling more calm now that he was cooler, sat down and rested his back and head against the earthy bank. It was good to be still. The Little Princess sat down by his feet.

Amy, who had also peeled off her jacket, settled herself alongside him, and began stealing furtive looks at the princess, who gazed into the distance as if somehow removed from their company.

"Remember that headset, with a sort of mask on the front?" asked Chris. "You looked as if you were going to put it on."

"Yes," answered Amy. "So?"

"People wear stuff like that in virtual reality situations."

"I sort of understand what virtual reality is – not properly though; not all the technology behind it. But why are you talking about it now when –"

"Well, it's the only thing that seems like it could explain what's happened to us." Chris was frowning. "And yet not . . . You see, virtual reality doesn't actually transport you anywhere, it just allows you to *feel* as if you're somewhere by computer simulation. Sometimes it's done through sound and vision coming through a headset like that one you picked up."

"But I still don't get why you're talking about this." Amy was frowning, too. "I didn't put that mask on. And, anyway, even if I had, that wouldn't affect *you*." She pointed at the Little Princess. "Or her. And she's *real*. This isn't a computer-simulated place, is it? Look!" Amy picked up a handful of grass and leaves. "We aren't seeing these through some sort of lens. They're real leaves and real grass. We didn't hear those arrows through anything either." She nodded towards the princess. "She's here. *We're* actually here, in this place, wherever it is. So how did we get here?"

"I know everything around us is real," agreed Chris. "I'm just wondering if Uncle Reg had . . . Well, I don't know really what I'm wondering." He nudged the Little Princess gently, indicating that she should open her hand. "And *this* is real," he said to Amy, as they both stared at the glowing jewel, almost too big for the princess's tiny hand.

The Little Princess looked into Chris's face. "The Seven Tunnels are next. Do you know which tunnel we have to go through?"

Chris saw the amazement on Amy's face. It was the first time she had heard the Little Princess speak. Maybe she had imagined that the tiny figure was voiceless.

31

"Don't worry," Chris told the princess. "I do know." He turned back to Amy. "We can't worry about how we got here. Not right now. We just have to accept that we *are* here and finish the game." He pointed at the Little Princess. "We have to look after her and get her back to her kingdom. The Seven Tunnels are part of the Sixth Mission."

AH, YOU'VE ARRIVED

Chris climbed to his feet and tied his jacket round his waist. "Let's go. The tunnels aren't far from here. In fact, I think I remember that they were just around this corner."

Reluctantly, Amy got to her feet and followed, muttering indignantly to herself. "This just makes no sense at all. One minute I'm in a room playing a computer and now . . . And you're going on about virtual reality, saying it's *not* virtual reality and . . . "

As her voice began to rise in pitch and volume, Chris broke in. "Amy! I don't know what's happening either. Well, I might have an idea, but I don't know *why*. The point is," and he waved an arm, "all this is real and we just have to deal with it. We have to carry on the game and accomplish the missions. Don't you see, if I hadn't cut the drawbridge down, the guards would have got us –"

It was Amy who interrupted him now. "Guards! What are you talking about?"

With a jolt, Chris realised that she hadn't seen the guards, either on the screen or in reality. She had appeared behind him and the Little Princess only when they were fleeing from the castle. Well, she was lucky. He had to admit he was still worried the guards might somehow cross the moat and come after them.

"Amy, please, just do what I say till we get a bit further on."

"I don't get it. The more I think about it, the more I don't get it!"

Chris had known Amy for years and her need to know what was happening, to understand it totally, was nothing new to him. It was part of the way she was. She had to get to the bottom of everything, from a maths problem to the reason why a cake hadn't risen. Then she either filed the information in her brain, in case it was needed again, or took immediate action, using what she had just learned. Right now, he sensed her frustration at not being able to do either of those things. He felt some of that frustration, too, but it was overridden by his instinct to keep moving on.

"Please, Amy. I'll do everything I can to look

after you." The minute he said it, he knew it was the wrong thing to say. Amy had always been fiercely independent.

"What makes you think I can't look after myself?"

Her face was tight, but Chris could see there was less fight in it than usual. He decided that ignoring her last remark was the best strategy as they rounded a corner and saw a cliff face of almost white clay, rising several metres high and slanting to the west, just as Chris had remembered. At its base were seven tunnel entrances, each spaced a few metres from the next.

"Caves!" exclaimed Amy, her frustration forgotten as an edge of excitement crept into her voice. She had once gone caving with a friend's family and had raved about it for weeks.

"I guess you can call them caves. They're called tunnels in the game. Seven Tunnels."

"Did someone say we have to go through?" asked Amy. "What's on the other side?"

Chris answered her first question. "We *do* have to go through, and I know which tunnel will take us to the other side." He didn't answer her second question.

Chris shepherded the Little Princess towards the

middle entrance way and was relieved to hear Amy following. To the left side of the tunnel entrance, he bent to pick something up.

"What's that?" asked Amy. She could see the shining silver sphere, slightly smaller than a cricket ball, he was now holding in his hand. But why had he bothered to pick it out from the jumble of stones around it?

"It's one of those things that you can pick up in a computer game and it comes in very handy later. There's one other tunnel we could have gone through quite safely, but I wouldn't have found this there."

"But what does it do?"

"If I throw it, I can create fire."

"You can create fire, the princess can create lightning, but what good are either of those things?" snapped Amy.

"Animals are usually scared of fire. Maybe it'll help us get past the Mountain Beast."

Chris ignored the look of strained disbelief on Amy's face and tucked the silver ball away in his jeans pocket. Then, followed closely by the Little Princess, he led the way into the tunnel. "Follow us, Amy," he called, "and, whatever you do, don't go off into any of the tunnels on the side."

"It's so dark," cried the Little Princess, clutching Chris's hand more tightly as Amy shook her head in disgust, then turned to follow.

Chris walked briskly, affecting a confidence he didn't entirely feel. "Our eyes will adjust in a few moments. You'll be okay." He called behind him again. "Are you all right, Amy?"

"Uh-huh." Her voice sounded small and faint. "The stalactites are fantastic!"

"Try to keep up with us," Chris called. They were well inside now and his voice bounced back from the walls in a confused volley of echoes – *with us, with us, with us* . . . "Stay close so I know you're okay." *Okay, okay, okay* . . .

He heard Amy laugh and then call, "Okay", which set the echo going again. *Okay, okay, okay* . . .

"Have you seen the stalactites?" Amy asked, her voice now close behind him.

"I always get mixed up between the mites and the tites," he confessed.

"You just have to remember that the ones that hang from the roof – the ones that have to hold *tight* to stay there – are *stalactites*. See? And that leaves the ones on cave floors as *stalagmites*."

"Cunning way to remember," replied Chris, still striding confidently forward, ignoring any of the tunnels that ran off to either side of them. Again, Amy fell behind a little, peering this way and that into the gloom. Her attention was caught by an intriguing display of glow-worms at the entrance of a smaller tunnel running off to her left and she stepped forward into the smaller cavern, eager to be surrounded by the natural glowing light. It was like a miniature starlit sky.

As she rotated slowly, peering upwards, the smooth stone floor beneath her feet tilted, slightly at first, so that she wasn't even sure that it was happening. Perhaps, she thought vaguely, the turning was making her dizzy. Then, with a sudden violent movement, the floor angled suddenly and sharply downwards. Amy's feet slid with it for only a moment or two before she lost her balance and was sent sliding downwards on her bottom, so unexpectedly and with such speed that she didn't even think to cry out.

As suddenly as she had started sliding downwards, she stopped. A stray thought about Alice falling down a rabbit hole was banished when she again saw glow-worms above her, and heard a voice saying, "Ah, you've arrived. I've been waiting a long time for you."

He made it sound like a long-promised visit, but

Amy had never seen such a creature in her life before and she certainly hadn't chosen to call on him.

"Amy?" called Chris. "Did you hear what I said? If we were to go down that tunnel," and he indicated an opening running off to the right, "we'd get turned to stone."

He turned around. Behind him, the Little Princess also inclined her exquisitely shaped head in the direction they had come.

"She's not here," said the princess.

"Amy!" called Chris, an icy alarm call racing through every limb. "Amy!" *Amy, Amy, Amy* . . . The echoes were his only answer. For, no matter how loudly, or in what direction, he called, no matter how wildly the echoes rang, there was no response.

"Perhaps she stopped to look at the glow-worms," suggested the Little Princess quietly. "They are further back."

Chris's panic subsided a little. "You could be right," he said, striding back down the tunnel as he spoke. "That'd be just like Amy. I didn't even notice any glow-worms."

Sure enough, the unearthly glow reached him

from a tunnel opening. "Amy! Are you there?"

There was still no response. Chris poked his head into the entrance and could see she wasn't there. If she *had* stopped to look at the glow-worms, surely she hadn't been tempted to go further inside after his warning.

At any rate, she couldn't have gone far. He could clearly see the end of this tunnel. In fact, it wasn't really a tunnel at all – just a deep hollow in the wall of the main tunnel. He looked down at the floor and saw writing running under his feet.

He stepped back and tried to interpret it: *parT diaM*. What did that mean? If it meant anything at all, that is. It looked like a meaningless jumble of letters. Perhaps it had been written a long time ago and some letters were now missing. Yet the lettering didn't look old.

"I wonder who wrote this," he murmured.

"An Underground Dragon," answered the Little Princess from just outside the small cavern Chris was standing in.

"A dragon! I didn't think dragons could write."

"It is the writing of an Underground Dragon. We have some of these dragons in my kingdom. They are the only dragons that can read and write."

"Really?" Chris decided to abandon that line of

enquiry and concentrate instead on the lettering. "Can you read this?" he asked the princess. "It doesn't mean anything to me." Was it his imagination, or had the floor tilted slightly?

"Maid Trap," replied the princess. "I would stand away from there if I were you."

Trap ... stand away ... The words made Chris leap back from the opening to join the Little Princess out in the tunnel. He stared long and hard at the words on the stone floor, until all at once he saw it.

"Ahhhh! *parT diaM*. Maid Trap. These dragons read and write backwards?"

"Yes," said the princess patiently, as if making allowances for someone who was regrettably slow on the uptake.

"You don't think that the words are a warning about an actual trap, do you? Could Amy have been trapped by one of these dragons?"

"Of course."

"Of course? You mean Amy could be somewhere with a dragon – trapped! And you stand there saying 'of course' as if you don't mind!"

"I merely wish to get to my kingdom. I do not wish to be held up longer than I need to be."

Chris glowered at the Little Princess. Was she suggesting that they go on without Amy? How dare she! Neither he nor Amy had made a conscious choice to be here. All they had done was choose to play a game, but here they were, doing all they could to get the Little Princess back to her kingdom. Perhaps it was pointless to expect gratitude, but there was no way he was leaving Amy behind, and certainly not in the clutches of a dragon.

Chris took the Little Princess's hand and bent down to look into her perfect little face. "We are going to find Amy immediately!" Even to himself, he sounded like a particularly bossy school teacher. He softened his tone. "Please tell me everything you know about Underground Dragons so that I can think of the best plan to deal with this situation."

"They read and write," said the Little Princess, staring at a point somewhere over Chris's head.

She had already told him that. He hardly needed to hear it again. Was she being ever so slightly insolent?

Chris decided not to challenge her. "Yes, and . . ." he said, making an effort to sound patient.

Now the princess turned to look at him. "They are not very big."

"Good. How big though?"

The princess looked him up and down. "Almost from your feet to your shoulders."

"They stand up then?" queried Chris.

"When they aren't lying down."

Chris gritted his teeth. "Really?"

The princess nodded solemnly.

"Are they fierce?" Chris asked. "Will Amy be all right?"

"They are lazy, unpleasant creatures. They are not frightening."

"What sort of unpleasant?"

"They smell," said the princess and wrinkled up her pretty little nose.

"Is that all?" Chris felt relieved. "So why do you think one has Amy? Why would he want to trap her?"

The princess waved an arm at the writing on the cavern floor. "As it says. He wants a maid."

Chris had a sudden desire to laugh. Amy wasn't the subservient type. She wouldn't easily agree – if she had any say in the matter – to be someone's maid, especially if that someone was a lazy, benign dragon.

"Okay, so how do we find this dragon? Do we have to fall into the trap ourselves, on purpose?"

"Certainly not!" The princess's tone sharpened considerably and she began to smooth her dress, as if she might ruffle it simply by thinking of such a thing.

"Well, how? You said you know about dragons." Chris was becoming impatient.

The Little Princess turned, walked the few steps across the main tunnel and pointed. "This is probably his entrance."

There was a small hole low down in the wall. Chris calculated that, though the princess could undoubtedly fit through easily enough, he would have a tight squeeze. But he was prepared to give it a go. "Let's go then. I'll follow you."

The princess looked him squarely in the face. "I am not going in." She said the words very firmly.

"But why not? I will need your help since you know about these dragons. You said they aren't frightening, just smelly. You said they're not even very big."

The determined look on the princess's face did not alter.

"If you don't come with me, you'll be sitting here all alone while I'm gone. You don't like the dark much, do you?"

"I will sit near the glow-worms and wait for you."

Chris tried to sort through the confusion of his feelings: anger with the Little Princess, worry about Amy, apprehension about dealing with a very odd-sounding creature. There was also a small but real fear that he could get stuck in the entrance leading to the dragon's lair. Never in his life had he had to worry about something as crazy as the possibility of getting stuck in the entrance to a dragon's cave. How, how, how had all this come about?

5
TRY A RIDDLE

Chris strode over to the hole, got on his hands and knees and put his head inside it. Beyond the narrow entrance it widened out into a long, high tunnel. Relieved, he pulled his head back.

"All right then," he told the Little Princess. "You wait here, but first tell me the best way to rescue Amy. A fight? A trick? What should I expect to have to do?"

As he spoke, Chris's sense of the absurdity of his predicament grew. Dragons, even small ones, weren't usually an issue in his day-to-day living.

The princess settled herself just outside the small cavern and began to smooth her skirt once more. "Try a riddle," she said.

"A riddle?"

"Yes, a riddle that he must answer correctly. Underground Dragons think they are very clever."

The expression on her face suggested that she thought otherwise.

Chris's brain whirred. He was supposed to make up a riddle and Amy would be the prize. Could he make up a riddle that was difficult enough? Maybe the princess was wrong and the dragon *was* clever. There was a good chance of that if it could read and write. What if the dragon gave the right answer?

It seemed that the princess had guessed his thoughts because she gave a tiny sigh and said, "If you have trouble, call me and I will come and help you."

Chris had mixed feelings about this unlikely offer but, nevertheless, he found he *was* feeling a little more confident. "Thanks," he muttered.

The Little Princess tilted her head back and stared wordlessly up at the glow-worms.

"I'm going now then."

The princess continued to stare upwards.

"Well, I suppose I can take it that it's not a mission of great danger," muttered Chris. "You certainly don't seem worried."

He got down and began wriggling through the hole. It was a tight fit and he hoped he didn't have to make a hasty escape from an angry dragon on the other side.

But he got through without incident and was at least ten paces down the long, high tunnel when he saw more writing in the same style he had seen back in the cavern: *EriuqsE kirE fo emoh.*

This time Chris was able to read it. Erik seemed an unusual name for a dragon. An arrow pointed from the wall sign to a door in the rock wall and, before he could lose his nerve, Chris knocked.

The door opened so promptly and so suddenly that Chris was startled but it was the smell that made him step back. No wonder the Little Princess hadn't wanted to come with him! Unpleasant was far too mild a word to describe the odour that seemed to issue from the dragon that confronted him.

"Come in, sir. Come in." Erik Esquire, the Underground Dragon, was beckoning with a greenish-brown clawed hand. (Was it correct to call the appendage on a dragon's foreleg a hand?)

Chris turned his head, took a last great gulp of fresh air and stepped inside. The Little Princess's description of this odd creature had been accurate, as far as it went. The height was about right. Its body shape, as one might expect of a dragon, was solid rather than slender. Its back and limbs were covered in a mix of brown and green scales, its underbelly was smooth-skinned and an unhealthy white.

Chris had never thought of a dragon as a smiling creature but this short-nosed specimen was definitely grinning at him, displaying crooked teeth splayed at odd angles. Combined with the grin, the googly eyes blinking from behind a pair of glasses gave him a decidedly unthreatening appearance. Instead, he had, thought Chris, a goofy look.

Having taken all this in at a glance, he was about to examine the creature further when a voice cried, "Chris! I am so glad to see you!"

"Aha!" said Erik, smiling even more broadly as he turned towards the sound. "You know each other. She has just taken a position here as a maid," he continued, turning back to Chris. "She's still getting used to the job."

"I will never 'get used to the job', as you put it. I am *not* your maid and I never will be!"

Chris's relief at hearing that Amy's voice was as full of fire and fury as ever turned to shock when he saw the metal bracelet around her ankle and the chain that attached it to a sturdy table leg. The table itself was littered with books and dishes and half-eaten food. In fact, the whole of the large room was littered in a similar fashion.

Chris was delighted to see her, though he couldn't resist teasing her. "Actually it does look as if he needs a maid," he said, indicating the untidy room.

"Well, I'm not it! I came down that chute over there," said Amy sulkily, pointing to the corner of the room, "and before I could collect my wits, he had this on me." She pointed to the chain. "I will not be a maid for anyone, least of all a smelly dragon!"

Chris cast a quick glance towards the dragon, wondering how he coped with insults, but he didn't appear to mind.

"She'll get used to being here, you know," said Erik, spitting a little as he spoke. "I'm not a mean employer. I'll feed and clothe her and, when everything is tidy and clean of an evening, I'll be only too happy to lend her my books to read."

Amy snorted. "They're written backwards!"

"Hardly! It's *yours* that are written backwards. I've seen some of your so-called books and it's *ours* that are written the right way round."

Amy didn't bother to answer this, and confined herself to making a scornful face, which Chris noted with some relief. It seemed the princess had been right to say the dragon wasn't frightening. And now he must get on with what he had come to do – freeing Amy. He just hoped that the horrible smell wouldn't affect his concentration.

He turned to the Underground Dragon. "Erik,

I'm told you're very clever."

The dragon smiled broadly. "I read a lot, you know. I've picked up a fair bit of knowledge in my time."

"I'm surprised then that you would chain someone up," said Chris carefully. "I'd have thought you would have read about the wise and fair treatment of employees."

Erik's smile faded. "I haven't hurt her, you know. I wouldn't do that. You might describe this tethering as a discipline. *You* probably do it with dogs. *We* do it with people – if we need to, you know. As soon as she shows she's reasonable and prepared to do the job, I'll take the chain off."

"I see," said Chris.

"I don't!" snapped Amy. "I want this off *now*. Chris, the key's on the shelf behind you."

Even as Chris turned, Erik was crossing the room in a single bound. He snatched the key up from the shelf.

Chris pretended he wasn't interested in this leaping and snatching and wandered over to the bulging bookshelf. "Do you read a lot, Erik? What sort of books are your favourites?"

The dragon's goofy grin returned. "I like epic adventures, tales of dragon derring-do! They're my most favourite. I also enjoy a little botany. I don't see plants a lot, living underground –"

"Well, why don't you live somewhere else then?" yelled Amy.

The dragon ignored her. "So I like reading about them and looking at pictures of flowers and trees. I enjoy a bit of geography, too. It's good to know about the world we live in."

"You don't live in it," hissed Amy. "You live *under* it."

Again, the dragon ignored her. "And I love riddles and crosswords."

"So do I," said Chris. Out of the corner of his eye he saw Amy's eyebrows shoot up in surprise. "Tell you what, Erik. Let's have a bit of a game. I'll ask you a riddle and you see if you can answer it."

The dragon's eyes positively sparkled behind his spectacles. "All right. I'm good at riddles."

"If you can answer it, I'll give you . . ." Chris made a show of searching his pockets and finding nothing, though the shape of the Fire Sphere could be plainly seen by anyone who was really looking. Quickly, he undid his belt and waved it at the myopic dragon. "I'll give you this! But, if you can't answer it, you can give me . . ." Chris scanned the room, as if puzzling over a possible choice. Just as the dragon opened his mouth to suggest something, Chris said, "I know! You can give me her." He pointed at Amy.

The dragon frowned, wrinkling up his snout so much that he knocked off his glasses and was forced to rescue them.

"Well, I can see she's a nuisance really," continued Chris, as the dragon propped his spectacles back on his nose and squinted at Amy. "She doesn't do anything, does she? Look at all this – she should be tidying it up. I'll take her off your hands and you can wait for another maid to fall into your trap."

The dragon looked doubtful.

"Of course, if you aren't really that clever . . ."

"I am," protested the dragon. "Ask your riddle."

Chris held out the belt again. "This is yours if you can answer." He pointed at Amy. "She's mine if you can't answer."

"Ask me! Ask me!"

"If you had a container that held five litres of water and a container that held three litres of water, how would you measure out one litre of water and know that you had exactly the right amount?"

"Aha," said Erik. "Aha." He sat down on top of a muddled heap of books in a large armchair. "I'll just need to think about it for a minute."

"Of course you will," agreed Chris.

He could see that Amy's defiant air had disappeared. She was nervous, he realised. He was nervous, too, but he hadn't seen any book on the dragon's shelf that related to maths. Nor had he made any mention of maths and logic as something he was interested in. Chris turned his back to Amy so that she could see his fingers crossed behind it. Thank goodness the Little Princess had suggested a riddle!

The dragon got up and began pacing about the room. When he stopped in front of Amy, she snapped, "Don't stare at me", sending the dragon's scaly snout into an outburst of twitching that dislodged his glasses again. Chris frowned at her. He didn't want the dragon upset.

The seconds ticked by and at last Chris said gently, "Okay, Erik. A clever chap like you must have the answer by now."

The dragon glared at him through eyes that had turned slightly red. "I haven't got the answer. Maths is not my strong point."

"Well then," said Chris. "Hand her over."

The dragon picked up the key he had placed on the table a minute before. He looked at Amy and then at Chris. "No," he said. "I won't."

"Come on, Erik. Fair's fair." Chris was determined not to show just how nervous he felt. After the challenges he'd already faced, and faced successfully, he had backed himself to deal with a short-sighted, short-legged dragon who seemed more dopey than dreadful. Surely he hadn't misjudged him.

Chris glanced at Amy and saw fear in her eyes – fear that maybe she was going to remain a prisoner in this foul-smelling dragon's lair. Chris knew he couldn't make a mistake now.

He strode to the door and pulled it open. Behind him the dragon was openly gloating. "Leaving already, are we? Goody, goody."

Chris thrust his head out into the tunnel and shouted, "Come now! Please!"

By the time he had slammed the door and come back to confront the dragon, Erik had lost his triumphant smirk and was looking rather confused.

"I am not leaving!" shouted Chris, putting his face as close to the dragon's spittle-flecked snout as he could bear. "Not without Amy! You couldn't answer the riddle and so I'm the winner. Hand her over!"

At that moment there was a rap on the door. Apparently pleased by the diversion, the dragon rushed over and flung it open. There was an odd little sound that Chris supposed indicated surprise and the Little Princess came into view, a small lace handkerchief held to her diminutive nose.

To Chris's astonishment, the dragon bowed and, in the meekest of tones, murmured, "Your Highness, I welcome you."

Chris glanced over at Amy. She, too, was now looking more astonished than fearful.

"Erik," said the princess, making no further progress through the doorway. "Your present visitors are my companions. I hope you have treated them well. However, it is time now for them to continue with me on our journey."

"Yes, Your Highness." Erik bowed his head again as he spoke.

Of course, thought Chris. The princess had said

that Underground Dragons lived in her kingdom. Erik must once have been one of them. How impressively dutiful he looked, with his scaly head lowered in front of the Little Princess. There was no doubt he was in awe of his ruler.

"Little Princess," said Chris. "We were coming back to you but Erik has chained Amy here." The dragon turned and glared at him. "He agreed to let her go if he couldn't answer a riddle, and he couldn't, but –"

"I'm still thinking about it!" protested the dragon.

"Erik!" said the princess sharply. "Undo the chain now."

"But –"

"*Now*, Erik! You don't want to find your relatives turned out of my kingdom – which I am on my way to right now – because you have been dishonest and then disobedient, do you?"

All defiance gone, the dragon slumped into himself until he seemed no more than half of his former height. He shuffled past Chris without looking at him, produced the key and unlocked the shackle on Amy's ankle.

Amy glared at him. "I won't say thank you! You should never have done such a thing in the first place." She strode over to Chris. "Let's get out of here!"

As they both turned away from the door to follow the Little Princess back to the narrow exit, the dejected dragon poked his head out behind them. "I still don't know the answer to that riddle. You didn't tell me."

"Work it out yourself if you think you're so clever," muttered Amy, without turning to look back at him.

The Little Princess turned round for a moment before she stepped through the entrance back into the main tunnel. "And, Erik, get rid of that trap."

"Yes, Your Highness," Chris heard him say meekly as Amy and then he squeezed through the hole behind her.

As they set off down the main tunnel once more, Chris thanked the Little Princess for coming to their aid.

"They only think they're clever," said the Little Princess, without looking at him. "He had no business holding up my return."

"None at all," agreed Chris. He turned away from her perfectly expressionless little profile to address Amy. "I'm glad to see you aren't wandering off anywhere now."

"I am *so* glad to be out of that place. He may

not have been a scary dragon, but he was *extremely* smelly. I was so glad to see you appear at the door!"

"Glad to do it," said Chris, "but you have to promise me you won't go off to the side anywhere else here." He pointed to a tunnel he knew from past experience. "Down there, for example, is another place where you can turn to stone, and I've got no idea how to rescue you from that fate."

There was no response from Amy or the Little Princess, so Chris, too, lapsed into silence, broken only by their three sets of feet making an eerie, hollow sound on the tunnel floor. Chris was making the most noise of all. He rose on his toes to go more quietly by the next entrance. "Sssshhhh," he whispered to the Little Princess. "The Green Dragon's down that one!"

Amy gave a squeak of alarm.

"It's all right as long as we don't go down his tunnel," whispered Chris, with his finger to his lips to warn her to keep her voice down. "Thank goodness he wasn't the one who trapped you. He's fierce!"

"Why are there dragons everywhere?" hissed Amy.

"A computer game can have anything in it, including dragons, and, whether you're prepared to admit it or not, this *is* a computer game."

"I'm prepared to admit it," said Amy, in a

voice that sounded almost as meek as Erik's when confronted by the princess. "Though I still don't understand how we got here, I *do* understand that we have to keep going. Like you said, we have to keep playing to the end."

The winding tunnel seemed to go on and on and on and Chris's anxiety levels began to rise even higher. He remembered the screen fight he had once fought with the Green Dragon. And what if the guards had found a way over the moat and were even now catching up with them? The encounter with the Underground Dragon had wasted a lot of time, and, if the guards did catch up, it would be impossible for him to fight them all at once.

Remembering the Fire Sphere, he curled his hand around it, ready to roll it fast and hard. But, if he used it against the guards – and he had no idea if he might need to – he wouldn't have it to use against the Mountain Beast. And how would he pass the Mountain Beast without it?

"Are we nearly there?" Some tiny change in the princess's voice told him she was worried, too.

"Yes," said Chris, affecting a confidence he didn't

feel. "We're nearly there."

Around the next bend, Chris could see, to his great relief, a gleam of light piercing the blackness. The three of them ran towards it and out through the entrance, where they were greeted by soft green grass and a bank strewn with tiny blue and white flowers. At first, the sunlight was nearly blinding, but its warmth was consoling after the dank darkness of the tunnels.

Amy threw herself face down onto the sun-warmed grass and when she spoke, her voice was muffled. "Am I glad to be out of there!" She sat up and fixed Chris with a solemn stare. "Thank you for rescuing me."

Embarrassed, Chris pulled a face and tried to laugh it off. "Well, uh, just make sure you do the same for me if you have to."

"I will." Amy plucked a small starry flower and handed it to the Little Princess. "And thank *you*, too. I'm very, very grateful to you."

"An Underground Dragon can be a time-wasting being," said the Little Princess, apparently unmoved by either Amy's unpleasant experience or her gratitude. But she took the offered flower and sat down next to her. "These flowers are beautiful. I have beautiful flowers in my kingdom, too."

It was time now to think of what lay ahead, and Chris walked a few steps on to where a gaping ravine fell away from the flower-strewn bank. This, he knew, was only the first. There were six more chasms beyond this one.

He had leapt across the seven, deep, wide chasms before – seated comfortably at his computer. It was something else again to actually contemplate doing it – really jumping into the air and having faith that he could reach the other side. He could carry the Little Princess on his back to get her across – assuming that *he* got across, but how would Amy manage? She was fit, but her legs weren't as long as his. Would that matter? Could she jump as often and as far as she needed to? Could he?

Though his mind churned with worry, Chris sensed something moving and glanced back the way he had come. Above the tunnel from which they had just emerged rose a scrubby hill; the Wild Critters were racing down it! Chris ran back towards Amy and the Little Princess.

The Little Princess gave a sudden, piercing shriek as she, too, caught sight of the Wild Critters. "Quickly!" she said, her voice growing slightly louder in volume. "We must go!"

"What are they, Chris?" gasped Amy.

"Wild Critters. They're – well, they're a sort of dog," Chris lied.

The Wild Critters, he knew, were fearsome animals – part-dragon, part-lion. They were hunters, probably sent by the guards from the castle after he and Amy and the Little Princess had fled. He had been worrying about the guards pursuing them and had never stopped to consider that they might choose to use these awful beasts to hunt them down instead. Even at this distance, he could clearly see their red, glaring eyes and slavering tongues, and they were coming closer by the minute. As live creatures, these Wild Critters were truly terrible!

"Dogs!" protested Amy. "They're not like any dogs *I've* ever seen! What sort of dogs?"

Chris felt helpless. This was no time for discussion or explanation. This terrifying army of beasts would be on them in moments and he needed those moments to concentrate, to consider how he might stop them. Was there enough time to do anything?

As he stood, still unable to think or move, the Little Princess clutched at his hand. In her other hand she held out the jewel. Her fingers closed over it, then opened as she tossed the jewel into the air. Again and again she threw it – three times.

Suddenly, with the Wild Critters so close Chris

could hear the rasping of their breathing and see the greed in their eyes, lightning flashed in a searing bolt from the princess's jewel. It tore into the sky, glowing white-hot in the bright sunlight, and cracked with the sound of a stockman's whip above the Wild Critters.

Chris could not tell if it had scorched them or not, but he could see that their progress had at least been interrupted. They froze, almost as if they were one animal, and huddled together against the hillside, yelping. Chris hoped that the sight and sound of the lightning would be enough to halt them permanently, but he couldn't be sure of it. He must act.

"On my back!" he cried, and the Little Princess leapt up without a murmur, her tiny hands grasping his shoulders firmly.

"Follow me!" Chris told Amy. "Don't look behind, and definitely not down. Just look at me and follow! Do what I do!"

Chris ran. He ran through the flowers with short, fast steps and then lengthened his stride to take three long steps before the edge of the first chasm.

He soared high in the air. Below him, the gaping void beckoned and his head swirled as though it were a bowl full of dizzying stars. Then his feet met solid ground and he was clutching at a rocky spur to stop himself from sliding back and down into the blackness.

He hung for a moment, the Little Princess still clinging tightly to his back, his feet scrambling for leverage, until at last he could push himself up onto a more level strip of grass-covered earth. The Little Princess slid down from his back and stood beside him as they looked back across the chasm to where they had come from. The Wild Critters were baying now, their strange cries filling the air. Whatever effect the lightning had had on them, it seemed to be lessening. They were again in pursuit.

Amy was still over there. Chris had heard her running close behind him. Obviously she hadn't dared to jump, and he believed he knew why. She must have looked down into the terrifying blackness he had just cleared.

"I don't think I can do it!" called Amy.

"You have to do it," shrieked Chris.

"The critters will get you! Jump *now*!" It was the Little Princess, and she had never sounded more animated. It was the first time she had given an order to Amy. She was holding out the jewel again, her hand opening and closing.

Chris slid his own hand into his pocket and

closed it around the Fire Sphere. He could use it only once and he had hoped to keep it for defence against the Mountain Beast, but it was needed. He couldn't leave Amy behind for the Wild Critters to savage. If only he could turn the game off, as he might have done had he been playing on the computer.

"They'll jump!" cried the Little Princess. "I know they can jump!" She was throwing the jewel high into the air now and, in the flash of lightning that followed, Chris thought he glimpsed Amy running down the edge of the chasm, perhaps trying to gain speed to leap. He hoped so.

The lightning tore across the sky above the Wild Critters and they drew back as they had before. Now Chris hurled the Fire Sphere with every ounce of energy he could muster. It arced through the air like a falling star, and hit the ground in front of the animal pack before exploding in a burst of fire.

At almost the same moment, Amy leapt and landed not far from where Chris and the princess stood. She fell, half-sobbing, and then struggled back to her feet and stared behind her, amazed that she had managed to jump the chasm at all. Mostly she stared in abject fear that the Wild Critters were following.

They weren't. The creatures had divided at last

and were fleeing back up the hill with the flames following them. But Chris and the Little Princess didn't stop to watch. Instead, the Little Princess again jumped onto Chris's back, and he began to run, powered by fear, desperation and a renewed desire to win.

"Follow!" he called to Amy. "Follow!"

CLIMB NOW!

Chris leapt over the second chasm, and the third. Without hesitation now, Amy followed immediately behind him. Soon they had cleared the fourth chasm, and the fifth. Each time he leapt, Chris felt his head swirl as he passed over the blackness below, and each time he felt a surge of elation as his feet struck solid ground again.

Instead of looking downwards, Amy kept her eyes on the Little Princess clutching tightly to Chris's back. Once she had succeeded in leaping the first chasm, she had made herself believe, with all her heart, that she could do it again, and again – as many times as she had to.

"There are seven altogether," Chris yelled at one point, and Amy counted as she leapt. With only two more to go, fear that the strength in her legs would not last began to give way to a growing sense of elation. They had nearly made it!

Chris leapt the sixth chasm, clearing it by at least a metre, and Amy guessed that it probably wasn't as wide as the previous ones. It wasn't. She jumped with the same effort she had given to all the other yawning gaps and, like Chris, cleared it with a metre to spare. It was the first time in this mad sequence of events that she really felt excitement racing through her system. She would fly over the last one!

Amy watched Chris readjust the Little Princess on his back and then race forward and make the last leap. A smile broke over her face as he sailed into the air – up and over, and down.

Down! Too far down! He hadn't made the other side! He was disappearing below the level of the grassy edge!

"Chris!" shrieked Amy. "Chris!"

She had thought she might enjoy jumping the last chasm – perhaps relishing the feeling of being a winner in this game – but all sense of excitement was gone now, replaced by sheer need. She raced towards the lip of the void and leapt wildly across the last deep ravine. On the other side, she fell to her knees for a moment as she landed, then scrambled up again and ran the few steps to where Chris's hand clutched at a jutting rock just below the edge of the chasm. Her stomach lurched sickeningly as she looked down at the depths below him.

Suddenly, the Little Princess began scrambling up onto Chris's shoulders, pushing with her feet to try to lever herself up and over his head. Inspired by the sight of Amy up on the grass, she seemed to be trying to reach out to some foliage hanging just above her.

"Stay still!" Chris's face was pushed against the side of the ravine, his voice filled with panic. "Stay still!"

Amy flopped to the ground, her head now almost at the same level as the Little Princess's pale, distressed face. "Don't you dare move another centimetre!" Amy hissed. "Stay right where you are and stay *still!*"

"Amy, is that you?"

"Yes, it's me. Don't worry, I'm going to help you."

"I can't hang on much longer."

The princess squeaked in fright and Amy glared at her once more. "You heard me! If you want to get back to your kingdom, don't move! Chris, there's a rock just behind me. I'm going to hand you a rope and, if I straddle the rock, I'll be able to take the weight as you pull yourself up."

"A rope?" Chris's voice was filled with doubt, but Amy was already taking her jacket from around her waist, rolling it up and making a series of knots down the sleeves and one in the back.

"It's really my jacket, but it'll do the same job. Can you hold onto it with your other hand?"

"I think so. I've got one foot on a little ledge. I'll push off from that, but you'll have to hold really tight to that jacket. It won't rip, will it?"

"It's some synthetic thing. It's strong. Here." Amy dangled the end of one sleeve of the jacket over the chasm and gave the princess the nearest thing to a smile that she could manage. "You'll be out in a moment, Princess. Just hang on."

She let the jacket unroll as she stepped backwards to the rock jutting out of the grass. "Don't pull on it until I say."

Amy sat in the grass behind the rock with one leg on either side and looped the jacket around it. With both hands, she took a firm grip on the end of the other sleeve, just in front of the last knot, and drew her knees up so that her heels could dig into the ground for leverage.

"Okay, climb now!" she shouted.

Amy took a quick, deep breath, breathed out and held on for dear life – for her life, for Chris's life and for the Little Princess's life. They could all end up in the chasm if this didn't work.

Her knuckles whitened. The jacket material cut into her fingers and she felt herself being pulled forward and over the rock. As the rough surface dug into the soft tissue of her stomach, a cry of fear from Chris nearly made her lose her hold. He hadn't fallen, had he? He mustn't fall! She must hang on. She no longer felt the rock digging into her stomach. The only thing she could think of was the only important thing – hanging on.

Suddenly, the dreadful pressure eased a little and the Little Princess flopped onto the ground beside her, as if she had fallen out of the sky. As Chris pulled his way out of the ravine, she had launched herself over his head to drop onto the longed-for comfort of solid ground. Within a few seconds, Chris, too, was lying beside them, groaning face down on the grass.

The jacket was slack in Amy's hands now and she flung it aside to scramble towards her cousin. "Are you all right?"

"I'm fine. I'm fine. I'm just groaning with relief. You've no idea how long I seemed to be hanging there." Chris rolled over and stared up at the wide blue sky above him. "That is the most marvellous sight I've seen in my entire life. Amy, you're a star!"

"Well, you rescued me. So now I've rescued you." Amy grinned at him and Chris grinned back. "We're even now."

For a minute or two, they sat under the sunny sky and enjoyed the solid ground beneath them and the flowers around them. They could have been relaxing in the safety of somebody's garden, not resting on the edge of dangerous territory.

Chris told Amy how he had felt the ledge crumble just as he pushed off. He had cried out, but it hadn't mattered in the end. It had given him enough leverage to transfer his weight to the jacket-rope. Amy told Chris how the rock had nearly cut her in half and they both examined the marks, which would soon turn into a large bruise.

"We must go on to my kingdom!" interrupted the Little Princess, her tiny face still pale, but impassive.

Amy rolled her eyes at Chris. "She's always saying that. She's what most makes me remember that this is a computer game. She's sort of . . . computerised. Most of the time she doesn't seem to have any feelings at all."

Chris shushed her with a frown.

Amy turned to the princess, who was staring blankly ahead of her. "I'm sure this has been a very scary experience for you as well as for Chris. I'm sorry I had to yell at you, but the whole point of this is to get you to your kingdom and falling down that chasm wasn't going to get you there. We'll be moving on in just a moment or two."

"We will," agreed Chris. He sat up and pointed ahead. "That's where we're going – across the sands to the Tower of Choices. There's nothing frightening in there."

Amy narrowed her eyes as she stared in the direction Chris was pointing. Far in the distance, she could see a burst of colour rising out of an expanse of shining, white sand. "This is the Seventh Mission, isn't it? The last one? I'm glad it's not scary."

"I didn't say that," countered Chris. "I just said that there's nothing frightening in the Tower of Choices." Then, before she could ask for further explanation, he got to his feet. "Come on, let's go."

The Tower of Choices came into sharper focus as Chris, the Little Princess and Amy approached it across a seemingly endless sea of white sand. It was roofed with squares of metal that danced with the vibrant colours Amy had seen earlier and its seven storeys were built of brick and criss-crossed wood panels. It was an imposing and intriguing sight, standing alone in its desert territory.

The walk across the fine, white sand had been difficult and they were all delighted when the end of a red brick pathway appeared, leading to the tower's entrance. The paving felt firm and much easier to walk on.

As they approached the huge, ancient-looking door, however, Amy hesitated and stopped. "The Mountain Beast doesn't live in here, does it?"

"No, no," insisted Chris. "I told you, there's nothing scary in here."

On the door there was a gold frame enclosing a statement written in an elegant hand in gold and black inks. Chris read the words aloud:

Stop here, Traveller, and rejoice.
This tower is filled with many a choice.
Three of these are all you need.
Take no more because of greed!
Then continue on your way,
And may Good Fortune light your day.

The heavy door creaked as Chris slowly pushed it open to reveal a smooth wooden floor patterned by light falling through the criss-crossed panels.

"Cupboards," said Amy, staring around her. "Nothing but cupboards – and look at the handles."

The doors were crooked, hanging at odd angles. Some dangled from leather ties, some had been hung on ancient metal hinges. The handles were carved to resemble quaint little animal heads and Amy went from one to another, delighted by the variety and skill of their making.

"Gorgeous!" she exclaimed. "Look, there's even a unicorn! And here's a . . . well, I don't know what it is. Some other kind of mythical beast, I suppose." She looked across the room to Chris. "Are there more of these upstairs?"

"Heaps more. There are cupboards on every storey and, as the rhyme on the door says, we have to choose three of them to open. Just three."

Amy stroked the small head of a horse. "And there are things inside, I guess. What sort of things, Chris?"

"Well, if we're lucky we'll find things to help us on the rest of this mission." To himself, he added softly and fearfully, "The dreaded Seventh Mission."

Chris was well acquainted with fear. There had been many moments in his life when it had risen inside him and he knew there would be many more.

He was always filled with fear before an exam – an irrational fear that he wouldn't know the answers to any of the questions, and a more rational fear that he hadn't done as much study as he should have done. But he'd been able to banish those fears by immersing himself in the exam.

Sometimes he'd been overwhelmed by fear while attempting a climb on a rock face he'd never been on before, but there was always a rush of excitement to counter it. There was always his desire to conquer, to win. It could banish fear and replace it with determination.

"The seventh is the most important mission," he heard the Little Princess say beside him.

She was right, and to complete it, Chris had to let his will to win fuel his determination and subdue his fear. He must immerse himself in the task ahead.

"What sort of things will we find here?" Amy's voice held a note of suspicion.

"Could be anything from a jug to a juniper berry," answered Chris brightly. "It's a gamble. We need to find objects that will help us on the rest of this mission, but there's no way of knowing exactly what we'll find." He was circling the room now, touching this cupboard and that. "What we need most of all is a great big bundle of luck! Enough luck to bring up three really useful things."

"Such as?"

"Well, for one thing, I'd like some sort of weapon, since I've used the Fire Sphere," said Chris. "We're going to need something like that."

"You can do the choosing," said Amy firmly.

Chris guessed that she didn't want to be blamed if they found nothing useful. He knew she hadn't quite believed him when he told her there were no truly unpleasant surprises behind any of the cupboard doors.

"First, maybe we can sit down and rest. Is there a seat somewhere further up? My legs were still shaky from leaping those chasms and that's not even counting the long walk over the . . ."

"We can't stop," said Chris, his voice as firm as Amy's had been earlier. If he stopped now, the fear might creep back and he would lose his nerve altogether. He had to meet the Mountain Beast with fire and fight in his body. He had to *believe* he could win.

"I think we need time to talk." Amy studied her feet as if she preferred not to look at her cousin. "I'm sorry if I ranted a bit earlier on but I still don't understand where we are, or why. I mean, I don't even understand the arrows. Where *did* flying arrows come from?" She raised her eyes to look at Chris.

All Chris could tell her was how he had first realised he was in the game – the terror of real, life-sized guards above him, the smell of the damp castle walls, the sight of the dark waters of the moat below his feet. Amy nodded in understanding and he knew she was comparing his experiences to the terror of the tunnels and the chasms and the Wild Critters, and of being alone with the Underground Dragon.

Chris also talked about the thrill of winning each time they succeeded against huge odds, but he didn't tell her about the fear he felt of what was to come.

"I think maybe all of this is my fault for touching that cord," said Amy. "Maybe Uncle Reg really was some kind of genius and hadn't yet finished what he was developing. You know what I think? I think we've time travelled. Do you?"

Startled, Chris recalled the bookcase full of books about time travel. He shook his head, trying to clear it and bring to the surface his knowledge of the subject. Little came except the most obvious. "No! We couldn't have done that. We're not back in time, are we? And we're not in the future either. This is the same computer game that –"

"Please, I need to return to my kingdom,"

interrupted the Little Princess, fixing her pleading green eyes on Chris's face.

She was right. They had to keep moving on. Chris began to climb the stairs. "It's all right. We'll get you home. Come on, Amy. You can rest later. Time to make some choices."

THREE CHOICES

Stop here, Traveller, and rejoice.
This tower is filled with many a choice.
Three of these are all you need.
Take no more because of greed!
Then continue on your way,
And may Good Fortune light your day!

Chris led them up the tower, with Amy grumbling sarcastically as she climbed. "Oh, great! This is just what I needed after the lazy day we've been having – a little light exercise!"

At the very top, she fell silent, peering down through the lattice at the endless desert view while Chris debated his first choice. In the end, he counted out the seventh cupboard from the right-hand side of the door and pulled open the lion's head handle. Behind the door was a stack of drawers, so he counted downwards to the seventh one, took a deep breath and slowly pulled the drawer open. Amy and the Little Princess crowded in behind him to see what was in it.

At first they saw nothing, and then, right at the back of the drawer, they found a small stone bottle that looked as ancient as the huge door at the tower's entrance. It had a screw top made of a dull, grey metal.

"What is it?" asked Amy eagerly.

Chris took out the little bottle and read the words carved into the stone: *Health Vial.*

"What does that mean?" asked Amy, puzzled.

Chris unscrewed the top and tipped the bottle sideways. As the blue liquid moved in the jar, an unusual smell wafted out – a mix of cinnamon and lavender and something else he couldn't identify.

He screwed the top back on. "My guess is that it's some sort of healing potion. Maybe it'll be useful if any of us are hurt."

But it wasn't a weapon, he thought to himself. That was what he most needed. He slipped the vial into his pocket and, beckoning the princess and Amy to follow, ran back down the stairs.

Chris made his second choice from a cupboard directly opposite the ancient door at the bottom of the tower. This time there were shelves behind the cupboard door, all empty except for the top one. Chris picked up the object lying there. It was some sort of scroll.

"Is it a map?" asked Amy. "Do we need one to find the kingdom?"

"I know where my kingdom is," said the Little

Princess, with just a suggestion of rebuke.

"Maybe it's a charm that can vanquish danger?" continued Amy evenly, keen to show she was not chastened by the princess's tone.

"I doubt it," returned Chris as he unrolled it. A dark frown settled over his features.

"What is it? What is it?" Amy was becoming impatient.

Chris took a short breath and read out, in a dull tone, "Question: Where can you always find money? Answer: In the dictionary."

Now it was the Little Princess's turn to frown. A tiny line appeared between her sculpted brows. "What does that mean?" she asked.

Angrily, Chris threw the scroll aside. "It's a silly riddle. In fact, you couldn't even call it a riddle! It's supposed to be a joke, I guess. We don't need jokes."

"Perhaps it's supposed to cheer us up," said Amy, in an effort to comfort Chris. "Though I can't imagine it making anyone feel better," she added, her voice trailing off.

Abruptly, Chris began climbing back up the stairs until he came to a stop on the second floor. "There's a seat. Take a rest if you like," he said, as Amy and the Little Princess followed him into the room. Amy settled herself on a long, squat-legged bench and watched Chris circle the room, gloom etched on his face. The Little Princess remained by the door.

Eventually, Chris stopped circling and sat down beside Amy. "The fact is, I'm too scared to make the third choice. I was so sure we could win. But I haven't done too well so far, have I?"

"Well," replied Amy hesitantly, "the riddle wasn't any use, but the Health Vial might be."

Chris sighed. "You must have realised by now that the missions keep on getting more difficult." Amy nodded. "The rest of this mission is *very* difficult."

"We'll be okay." Amy put on her brightest tone. "Then it will all be over. We'll be able to go home. We will, won't we? Don't you think?"

"I certainly hope so," said Chris gloomily, "but I haven't a clue really. Maybe we'll have to stay here forever –"

"Don't say that!"

Fear was written all over her face and Chris recovered himself quickly. "Don't worry. I was only clowning around," he consoled her. But, he wondered, *would* they be trapped forever in this fantastical world – a world they had never chosen to enter?

"Of course we'll get home. Okay, last choice coming up!" He made the last words sound as cheerful as he could and leapt to his feet with a show of enthusiasm. He was glad to see the tide of fear begin to ebb in Amy's face.

Chris's last choice was on the fourth floor. He spun crazily around in the centre of the room and then, with his hand outstretched, staggered dizzily towards the wall until he connected with a cupboard.

"A pig! For crying out loud!" he complained, as his hand closed on the animal handle of the door.

There were no shelves or drawers in the tall, narrow cupboard. The final object Chris could take from the tower was tucked away at the back and he had to reach right in to draw it out.

It was a long stick, polished to a shiny brown, with a bulbous swelling on one end that made it easy to grasp. Chris stared at it as he ran it through his hands, then peered closely at each end, as if he might find a magic button that would turn it into a sword or release a lasso. There was nothing. It was simply a stick, shaped and polished, but still just a stick.

"It may as well be another joke! It *is* a joke! It would probably make a great walking stick for a little old man, but what use is that to us!"

"A walking stick can be a sort of weapon," suggested Amy doubtfully.

Chris didn't answer.

"It could have been something worse," said the Little Princess. "It could have been a snake or evil –"

"And it could have been something better," snapped Chris.

Despondently, he led them down the stairs and out of the tower. He needed to take time in this safe space to think. If he was to have any chance of passing the Mountain Beast, he had to be strong – more than strong. He had to have a plan, and either a super weapon or phenomenal strength.

But he had none of those. How was he going to be able to take the Little Princess any further? A tide of deep despair began to rise in him – grey and heavy, creeping through every corner of his being. Amy said nothing, and he was glad of that, but all the same, how he wished that she would suddenly announce some great plan or idea.

Eventually, the Little Princess's voice broke into his despair. "We are nearly at my kingdom." Again she was urging him on.

Chris rose reluctantly to his feet, fingering the Health Vial in his pocket. Oh, how he wished it were the Fire Sphere.

"Which way do we go now?" asked Amy, glad to be moving on. Maybe a little activity would help Chris regain a more positive attitude.

"We go past the Mountain Beast and on to my kingdom," answered the Little Princess when Chris didn't reply.

"But which way? North? South?"

Chris didn't even hear the question. His mind was still tussling with the problem of how he was going to get past the Mountain Beast. The problem seemed enormous and completely insoluble.

Amy persisted: "Do we go back along the brick path or –"

"It's no use!" declared Chris suddenly. He wheeled about and stared at the words on the door again.

Stop here, Traveller, and rejoice.
This tower is filled with many a choice.
Three of these are all you need.
Take no more because of greed!
Then continue on your way,
And may Good Fortune light your day.

He turned back to face Amy and the Little Princess. "I'm going back into the tower to make another choice."

The princess stared at him then recited, "*Three of these are all you need.*"

"She's right," said Amy, turning to the words in the frame and pointing at the fourth line. "Look: *Take no more because of greed!* It says that quite clearly."

"So?" Chris was defiant now. "It doesn't say the world is going to end if I do take another choice, does it?" he asked angrily. "I don't believe we'll all drop dead! Anyway, I'm not taking another choice because of greed. I'm taking another choice because of *need*!"

"Somehow it doesn't seem honest," said Amy. "It *seems* greedy, even if you don't mean it to be."

"You've got absolutely no idea what we're going to have to do battle with, have you?" Chris's voice was rising. "Ask the Little Princess! She knows. We have to get past a monster and I've got nothing that will help us!"

"A monster?" repeated Amy, a new wariness in her voice. "A true monster?"

"Yes! A monstrous creature that is chained on the path we have to take to her kingdom." Chris jabbed a finger in the direction of the Little Princess. "If you'd like to know, I'm plain scared. *That's* what sort of a monster it is! Actually, I'm flat out terrified, if I really think about it. So, if you don't mind, will you let me get on with making another choice that's more useful than a stick and a joke and a mini bottle of medicine!"

He opened the door with a final heave and disappeared into the tower. Amy didn't follow.

"He is wrong to do this," said the Little Princess.

"He seems to be feeling desperate. Tell me, is the Mountain Beast really so terrible?" asked Amy.

"Yes," said the princess. "It is terrible." Her tone of voice displayed no emotion; she might as well have been reading a shopping list. If it really *was* terrible, thought Amy desperately, surely the princess wouldn't be able to hide her fear of it entirely. Chris had been honest about his terror of the creature. It was what had driven him to return for another choice. But was the Mountain Beast actually as bad as he seemed to think? Her mind in a whirl, Amy followed Chris back into the tower.

She found him on the third floor, and apparently he'd had time to cool down. In fact, he seemed somewhat shamefaced. "I shouldn't have yelled at you," he muttered. "It's just, well . . ."

"You're worried." Amy finished his sentence for him. "It's okay. I've seen you throw the odd tantrum before and lived through it. I'll yell back if you make me mad enough."

Chris managed a small grin. That was the good thing about knowing someone so well. When you lost it, they didn't think you were some out of control jerk, and they didn't take it personally. They understood it was a temporary lapse. Amy understood that he only yelled if he felt he had a good reason.

The trouble was, he wasn't entirely sure now that his reason had entitled him to start yelling at Amy. "You're allowed to feel angry, and to yell about it sometimes," his mother had always said, "but don't yell at other people when it's *your* problem you're angry about."

Chris decided to make more of an effort to be friendly. "I'm going to try this cupboard," he told Amy. "There's a lion's head handle on it."

"That would be good luck, don't you think?"

"I hope so."

He opened the door and quickly drew out a long, narrow box coloured dark blue. Could it be a sword? He flipped open the lid and felt his stomach drop with frustrated disappointment. It was another scroll, but it did look much bigger than the previous scroll – its rolled length matched the entire length of the blue box. Surely it couldn't be just another riddle? Not on such a large piece of parchment.

Amy sensed his disappointment and spoke as cheerfully as she could. "Take it out. Open it. Maybe it will tell you how to cope with the Mountain Beast. You never know."

Chris picked up the roll of thick cream-coloured paper and unrolled it as Amy moved closer to see. Together, they looked at the large words at the head of the scroll, their eyes widening as they read:

THIS IS A PENALTY CHOICE

For a moment they stared at one another, dread written on both their faces, then they returned their eyes to the smaller print below the first statement.

YOU HAVE ALREADY HAD YOUR THREE CHOICES IN YOUR SEARCH FOR USEFUL OBJECTS. YOUR ONLY OPTION NOW IS TO TAKE ONE OF THE THREE CHOICES OFFERED BELOW.
1. LEAVE THE LITTLE PRINCESS TO GO ON ALONE.
2. GO BACK TO THE BEGINNING OF THE GAME AND START AGAIN.
3. TAKE THE LONG WAY TO THE VALLEY GUARDED BY THE MOUNTAIN BEAST.

"No . . . " murmured Chris softly, as his eyes

skimmed once again over the three impossible choices. "No, no."

He dropped the parchment to the floor and pulled open another cupboard. Inside it was another long, blue box, exactly like the one he had just opened. He wrenched open another door. Another long, blue box lay inside. He pulled open more cupboards in different parts of the room. In every one there was a long, blue box.

Chris knew there was no point in searching any other storey. Every cupboard would contain the same object. He made a noise between a groan and a whimper and sat down abruptly with his head in his hands. "I shouldn't have come back."

Amy was past worrying about whether or not Chris should have returned to the tower. She was thinking about the penalty choices. "Chris, we can't start over again."

"No," said Chris in a hollow voice. He picked up the scroll and looked again at the three choices offered. "And we can't leave the princess to go on alone either."

"Maybe not," said Amy.

Chris cast a quick glance in her direction. "*Definitely* not!" he said sharply. "She'll never get past the Mountain Beast."

"Then the only option is the last one. We have to take the long way to the valley."

The Little Princess was standing at the door now. "I told you it was wrong," she said. "We were nearly at my kingdom before."

Chris was sure he could read sadness in the tiny, exquisite face and he felt rebuked. As well as yelling at Amy he had disappointed the Little Princess. "I'm sorry," he mumbled. "I'm really sorry."

Amy was putting scrolls back into boxes and boxes back into cupboards. "I can't believe that these are now in every cupboard. I don't know how this could have been done," she muttered.

"It's a computer game," sighed Chris, a note of bitterness in his voice. "You can do anything with computers . . . or so they say."

RAJA BIRDS

"It seems darker all of a sudden," said Amy as the three of them headed down the stairway to the ground floor.

Chris was still shaking his head over his own stupidity. "I *know* I shouldn't have come in here. It was –"

"Oh, don't start going on, Chris!" Amy spoke briskly. "It seems that it *was* a stupid thing to do, but you *did* come in, it didn't help anyone, end of story. Now we've just got to get on with it."

"We were nearly at my kingdom before," repeated the Little Princess.

Amy's voice remained brisk. "We'll get there. It will just take a bit longer." Then, as they passed one of the criss-crossed wood panels on the ground floor, she gasped and stopped still. "Trees!" she exclaimed. "That's why it's darker."

Chris pushed open the tower door. Outside, the white desert had completely disappeared. A forest now surrounded them.

"I don't like it," said the Little Princess.

"I think it's rather beautiful," said Amy. "I was just taken aback, at first, to see it here, because it wasn't here before."

"Which way do we go? There's no obvious path," murmured Chris, closing the door behind them.

After a moment's indecision, he told Amy and the princess to wait and headed off around the tower. Seconds later, he reappeared after completing a full circle. "There's only one track away from here, so that has to be it. This way."

Together, they skirted halfway around the tower until a path appeared and Chris led them into the forest. The track was flat and relatively smooth, edged with ferns and mosses. On either side, trees towered over them, casting a deep shadow. Now and again, bars of sunlight arrowed down between the trunks.

The princess remained silent as they walked, but Amy was filled with chatter, partly, Chris deduced, in an effort to keep him feeling positive.

"It really is so beautiful here, don't you think? The trees are so tall! We won't get too hot with all this shade, yet there is some sunlight. Do you think there are animals in there?" She peered hopefully to either side of the track. "I think I prefer forest to desert. There are so many more possibilities."

Chris was still feeling furious with himself for his decision to return to the tower. He had allowed the disappointment of finding no useful weapon to turn to fear and then panic, and look what he had brought down on them. Who knew how far they might have to walk now. The Penalty Choice had said *the long way*.

But at least he could show Amy he was over his gloom and was going to be positive from now on. He darted ahead and, with a flourish, used the stick that had been one cause of his troubles to hold back a bunch of overhanging fern.

"Why thank you, sir," said Amy, grinning as she passed by. "Very gallant, I'm sure. I told you that stick would be useful in some way."

Chris bowed in acknowledgment and his mind flicked back to the Mountain Beast. What positive thing could you say about a creature like that?

"Do you know the one good thing about taking this long route?" he asked eventually. After a short pause, he answered himself. "It will be a longer time before we have to meet up with the Mountain Beast."

"True," replied Amy. "So we don't even need to think about it for a while. Hey, look, more sunlight, fewer trees."

Sure enough, the forest was thinning out and soon it was behind them. Only the occasional tree broke the monotony of the flat, grassy plain that surrounded them now. It wouldn't be the most inspiring landscape to hike through. What they saw in one minute, they would see more of in the next.

"And will you look at that!" exclaimed Chris.

Disconcertingly, the ribbon of track in front of them wound on and on across the plain until it disappeared, far in the distance, over the horizon.

"It certainly is *the long way*," said the princess.

"Sure looks like it," agreed Amy.

Suddenly, a rush of air passed directly above them, accompanied by a strange sound, and they all ducked instinctively. They were about to raise their heads when the movement and the sound were repeated.

"Down on the ground!" yelled Chris, pulling the Little Princess under a protective arm. He had no idea what had just happened.

When no further disturbance followed, Chris gingerly lifted his head and, seeing nothing, pulled himself up. "All clear, I think." The Little Princess sat up and straightened her crown.

Amy sat up, too. "What *was* that?"

Chris scanned the skies. "I don't know." Then, "Over there! Was it those?" Not far to the left of them, three large birds were circling.

"They're huge!" exclaimed Amy.

Chris squinted upwards. The sky was bright with sunlight. "Hard to tell their size from here. Look! They're coming this way again."

Sure enough, the brown birds had stopped wheeling and were headed straight towards them. The Little Princess got to her feet. "I don't wish to lie down again."

"You mightn't want to," muttered Amy, clutching her knees to her chin, "but I'd be ready just the same if I were you." She watched as the birds came towards them across the sky. "They are so huge! I've never seen birds as big as that!"

The birds resembled eagles in shape but they were much larger – a uniform soft coffee-brown colour all over. When the sun caught the angles of their wings, their plumage glinted gold.

"They are Raja Birds," declared the princess matter-of-factly, dusting down the front of her skirt. "They will not hurt us."

"Really?" said Chris. He and Amy crouched once

again as the birds flew over, shifting the air about their heads, but this time they dared to look up instead of covering their faces with their arms.

"Big beaks," said Chris, noting the powerful curves cutting through the air as the great birds whistled overhead.

"But their eyes weren't scary," said Amy.

"How could you see their eyes when they're going so fast?"

"The same way that you saw their beaks."

The birds turned and flew over them once again, this time a little higher, then glided gracefully downwards and settled on the ground not far away.

Reassured by the princess's words, Amy was intrigued rather than fearful. "What do you suppose they want?"

"I hope it's not us." Chris was still unnerved. Surely it was unusual for birds, especially of their great size, to hover so close to humans?

"They will not hurt us," repeated the princess.

"Do you have these birds in your kingdom?" asked Chris.

"Sometimes they come," replied the Little Princess. "Let us go on now. We have a long way to walk."

As they continued along the track, the three

birds periodically wheeled overhead and then glided down just ahead of them to sit watchfully as Chris, Amy and the princess passed.

"I'm sure they want something," Amy said more than once.

"What *I* want," Chris told her, a little irritably, "is to get to the end of this track." He was deeply concerned that this present flat terrain, tedious though it was, could change into something infinitely more challenging. He thought back to the Fourth Mission, completed when they were safely seated at the computer. There had been storms and landslides in steep and hazardous country. There had been giants and snakes. Maybe more such dangers lay ahead of them.

None of them talked much as they went on. It was hard to feel they were making any progress when the landscape was so unvarying, but the weariness of their legs told them they were.

Finally, something altered. Higher ground began to take shape on the horizon and the sight spurred them on.

"I am so pleased to see a different landform," said Chris. "I thought this plain would never end."

As they drew nearer, it became clear that what they were seeing was a high rock formation. It seemed to extend as far as the plain did, forming a sort of boundary.

"Maybe there is a tunnel through it," mused Amy. Chris noticed she didn't exclaim in delight at the possibility of caves, as she had when they had approached the white clay cliff.

When at last the track ended, slap-bang against the rock wall, there was no tunnel in sight.

"Good place for some challenging rock climbing," said Chris, keen to stay positive.

Amy murmured agreement without taking much notice. She was busy watching the birds, which were now perched on a rock jutting out low down on the cliff face. She noted the way the birds occasionally spread their wings slightly then drew themselves closer to the ground.

"Amy, what do you think?" Chris's voice brought Amy back to their immediate situation. "The track ends here so I guess we need to find a way over or under this. Help me look for a possible way."

They left the Little Princess waiting in the shade of the rock face as they wandered one way and then the other, but in neither direction could they find any way through it or over it. What they could see of the wall was solid, high and sheer. Fatigue from the long walk soon set in and they both suspected there was nothing to find anyway. They returned to the Little Princess.

"This is the only place where it looks even remotely possible to climb without a rope," said Amy, scanning the rock carefully.

"Like I said before," said Chris, "a good rock climbing place."

"Did you?"

Chris rolled his eyes. "You were too busy bird-watching to listen."

All at once, Amy was filled with determination. "Then that's what we do! We climb it. Right here. We're both good at rock climbing."

"I'm not," said the Little Princess.

10
DON'T LOOK DOWN

Amy and Chris didn't respond to the Little Princess's remark. Instead, they began to debate the practicalities of climbing the steep rock face before them. They had no rope to help them climb and keep safe, so it was important that they seek out the most secure possible route. They studied every rock protruding from the mainly smooth face, trying to decide where foot and handholds were within reach of each other.

At last, Chris noticed the suggestion of a frown on the Little Princess's face and assured her that she could ride on his back. "You won't have to climb yourself. Maybe we can make you a sling from our jackets to prevent you from leaning out the wrong way."

"Good idea," agreed Amy, remembering the way the princess had wriggled about on Chris's back at the chasms. "We don't want Chris losing his balance at some critical moment."

Chris could see that Amy believed the climb was achievable; she even seemed quite excited about it. But he couldn't help feeling worried himself. The face was high. Normally he wouldn't have considered climbing it without a rope or other climbing aids and no proper footwear. Should they be trying it at all?

Amy answered the question forming in his mind. "We have to get over it or go back and start again, Chris, and there's no way I'm going through six of those wretched missions, some of them for the second time!"

"We're nearly there," said the Little Princess, with a barely noticeable nod. Was she trying to encourage them?

Just in case, Amy nodded back. "You're right. We're nearly there."

Together, Chris and Amy plotted out the best possible route one last time, slightly altering an angle or two as they sighted better rocks to hold on to or to rest on. As they stared intently upwards, the three huge, coffee-coloured birds launched themselves from their rock and soared up to the top of the face. There they rested for a moment before flying into the sky and circling several times, then returning to their lower perch.

Amy couldn't help following their flight. "I wonder why they're doing that? Do you think it could be a demonstration, especially for us?"

Chris gave this suggestion the attention he thought it deserved and ignored it. "I don't want one of those things flying close when I'm concentrating on climbing. Anyway, I'm going to sit down here and rest for a bit before we start. We've been walking a long time and we need to refuel our energy."

"It would be good to have something to refuel it with," said Amy. "You know, we haven't eaten or drunk anything since we began all this. It hasn't seemed to matter till now. I could murder a glass of water."

"Well, there's nothing to drink here, so I'm afraid we'll have to do without."

"I guess I'll manage. Do you think when we make it to the top we'll be close to the valley where the Mountain Beast is waiting?"

Chris's stomach lurched. "Maybe."

"What's it like? You've never really said."

Chris was silent for a while. Then, just as Amy was about to speak again, he said, "Like nothing you've ever seen before. It's huge, it's scary and I can't really imagine how scary it's going to be as a real, living creature, not just a picture on a screen. I honestly don't know how we'll get past it, though it's the last and most difficult thing we'll have to do to get the Little Princess home to her kingdom. Climbing this," and Chris waved his arm at the rock face, "suddenly seems like nothing when I think of the Mountain Beast."

Amy was silent.

"It can't actually run very far after you," continued Chris, trying to think of the most positive aspect of the horrifying ordeal to come. "It's chained, you see. Chained on the path between the rocky valley sides. And the only way for us to get through is on the path where the beast is tethered."

Chris knew Amy would be trying to think the problem through, looking for an alternative approach, as though their problem were a mathematical one. He wished it were.

The Little Princess interrupted their thoughts. "Shall we go now?"

"Very soon," Chris assured her.

"When you played the game before," said Amy, "there was only you and the Little Princess. Now there's me as well. That could make a difference."

"How?"

"The valley slopes are not like this rock face, are they?"

"They aren't nearly as steep."

"Well, if the valley slopes aren't impossible to climb, maybe I could create a diversion, attract the beast's attention while you sneak around the side with the princess. What do you think?"

Chris felt a small spark of hope leap up in his heart. It was the first time he had been able even to imagine the possibility – even the tiniest possibility – of passing the Mountain Beast, with just a vial of unrecognisable medicine and a polished stick to help them.

"Maybe," he said cautiously, unwilling to show any real enthusiasm until he had had more time to think the idea through. "Maybe that could be possible."

"Shall we go now?" repeated the Little Princess.

"Okay," said Chris. He looked up at the rock face, running his eyes over the route they had chosen, and started to feel excited. He could do this! He could climb to the top and over.

And he might even be able to pass the ultimate obstacle, the Mountain Beast. With Amy's help he might actually win! And, he thought, remembering their recent adventures, the princess might be able to help, too. He had thought of himself as her protector, her bodyguard; he'd never really considered that she had helped him before, and still could. She had her jewel to make lightning. And that had easily turned the Wild Critters back.

He and Amy and the Little Princess . . . A surge of hope formed somewhere in the centre of his being and, slowly but surely, began flowing through him.

"On my back!" he cried to the princess. "We're on our way!"

"I thought you were going to make a sling from the jackets to help keep her steady on your back. I really think you should," warned Amy.

"She's very light. We'll be okay." Chris bent down and the Little Princess jumped on his back.

"I will hold tight," she said. "I will stay close like this," and she tucked herself in against Chris's back as though she were part of him.

"You'll have to stay exactly like that all the way up." Amy was still nervous about it. "You mustn't lean out in any direction, no matter which way Chris leans or bends."

"I know," said the Little Princess flatly, looking past Amy and into the distance. It seemed to be her way of ending any conversation she would rather not be part of.

Chris tossed the stick in Amy's direction. "I don't know if this will be of any use but maybe we should take it. Use your jacket to tie it on so it won't get in your way. I can't manage it and the princess."

"All right," said Amy, a little reluctantly. "Are you going to follow me, or will I follow you?"

"I'll go first. If the footholds are secure for me, you'll know they'll be fine for you coming after."

Chris began working his way up the face. It wasn't too difficult for an experienced rock climber, he decided, but it was challenging and he needed all the skills he could muster.

He moved slowly, testing each handhold, ensuring that it would later take his full weight as he moved upwards and used it as a foothold. Now and again, there was an indent or a crack where he could confidently get a firm grip. He preferred these to the small rocks that jutted out from the face. He double-checked each one of these, making utterly sure they were secure.

The Little Princess squirmed once or twice on his back but stayed close. "Remember, don't look down," Chris reminded her. Once she pointed out that they were going very slowly, but Chris told her it was the safest way to move and that they would reach the top eventually.

Hope and excitement drove him on. This was not an impossible task. He would win! He would win!

"Okay, Amy?" he called after a while.

"Okay," she called back.

"Think of the view at the top."

"I am," replied Amy.

Chris didn't find out until later what happened after that, and he was rather glad he hadn't. He didn't know how he would have responded to the sight of a snake suddenly poking its head out of a cavity in the rock as they climbed past it halfway up the face. As it was, the creature came eye to eye with the Little Princess, who was leaning her head on Chris's shoulder. All Chris knew was that the princess suddenly shrieked, and he felt her hold on him loosen.

"Hang on!" cried Chris, firming up his own grip on a deep cleft, keeping all points of his body as close as possible to the rock surface in front of him. But, even as he cried out, he knew it was pointless. The princess had already let go.

The next few seconds lengthened in the way time does at moments of extreme stress and confusion.

Chris heard the Little Princess cry out again, and Amy, too. There was a whistling, swooshing sound near him, and he felt the air moving. In front of him he could see only rock, and above him a glimpse of soft brown plumage against blue sky. These things were part of the whirling panic of knowing that the Little Princess had fallen.

Inwardly, he cursed the birds. They must have flown too close and startled the princess. His only option now was to remain where he was, glued into a position he knew he could maintain if the birds returned.

Then he heard Amy's voice, coming from somewhere closer to him than it had a minute or two before. "Chris, she's all right! One of the birds got her."

At first, Chris could comprehend only the last sentence. A bird had her! A bird had dived on the Little Princess and seized her!

"Chris, she's at the top now. A Raja Bird rescued her and carried her up! Keep going, Chris. Keep climbing."

Rescued her? It was too implausible to take in. Chris stayed where he was, rigid against the rock.

"Keep climbing, Chris! Go up!"

At last, he managed to start moving again. Hand

over hand, foot after foot, seeking a firm hold on the rock face. Up and up and up. And then he was there, pulling himself over the top, with Amy hauling herself over a few seconds after him.

"See," she panted. "She's here!"

Exhausted, he could only lift his head as he lay on the flat ground. The Little Princess was staring down at him, the ghost of a smile hovering on her lips.

"We should have let the Raja Birds bring all of us up," she said. "It would have been less effort for you."

A PREPOSTEROUS IDEA

It took some time for Chris's heart to slow to a normal rate after the panic of the last few minutes. He lay, face down, listening to Amy question the princess. Thank heavens he hadn't seen that snake.

Amy obviously wasn't interested in that. She moved quickly on from the snake. "What was it like being grabbed in the Raja Bird's beak? I saw it, you know. One minute you were falling, the next you were going back up! Hanging from the bird's beak by the band of your skirt. Did you know what was happening?"

"I was very glad to be saved," was all the princess wanted to say on the matter.

"Not scared?"

"Not of the Raja Bird, no."

Chris sat up. He found the conversation disturbing. He certainly didn't want to relive the moment when the Little Princess had let go as he climbed. Instead, he concentrated on the three Raja Birds perched on a small bank not far from them, and hoped they had now reached some place that was near the valley of the Mountain Beast. That would mean they were close to the princess's kingdom.

However, it didn't look as if they were anywhere near a valley. They seemed to be on a hill that sloped down to yet another huge plain, where another obvious track stretched into the distance. He groaned inwardly. Was the walking never going to end? Near the track he could see a tall stick with something white glinting at the top.

"I think I can see a signpost. I'm going down to see what it says." Chris got to his feet and walked slowly down to the bottom of the hill. As he drew closer, the sign came clearly into focus: *Distance to the Valley of the Mountain Beast – endless.*

What sort of sign was that? Did it actually mean what it said? *Endless*? It was difficult not to feel completely defeated.

Amy and the princess had followed him, with the Raja Birds flying close behind. All three landed with an easy elegance below the sign.

"Which one rescued you?" Amy asked the princess eagerly.

"Does it really matter?" asked Chris gloomily. "Read the sign, Amy."

Amy read and at first looked as defeated as Chris felt. Then all at once a smile lit her face. She turned again to the Little Princess. "When you said we should have let the Raja Birds take us to the top of the rock face, did you mean they *could* have done that?"

"Yes," answered the Little Princess.

Chris looked sceptical. "All dangling by our waistbands, I suppose."

The princess frowned at him. "In my kingdom, people sometimes ride *on* the Raja Birds, not hanging from them."

Amy went into an ecstasy of delight. "Truly? Really and truly? Why didn't you say so before?" Chris could see she was thinking of the many kilometres they had walked as a result of the Penalty Choice. Then he saw her eyes dart backwards and forwards between the birds and the princess, understanding dawning on her face. "Is that why they sit near us and sort of crouch and spread their wings? Are they inviting us to climb on? Are they?"

"Amy, that's hardly like–" Chris began.

But now the princess interrupted him. "Yes, they are."

Chris stared at her. "Really? You didn't tell us," he added accusingly.

"You didn't ask me," replied the Little Princess, her gaze drifting up and over his head, as if there was something very interesting far beyond him.

"That's it! That's our answer to this problem," exclaimed Amy. "We don't wear ourselves out walking. We fly!"

It seemed a preposterous idea. It seemed impossible, even dangerous. People didn't climb onto birds and fly away in order to get where they wanted to go – not even very large birds, not in the real world. Then Chris remembered that they *weren't* in the real world. They were in a computer game where anything could happen. Anything.

He looked over at the birds and, sure enough, they were doing just what Amy had described – crouching to lower their bodies, spreading their wings slightly. He hadn't noticed it before. But, if they all climbed on the birds' backs, how would the birds know where to take them?

"I know we didn't want to have this long diversion," continued Amy excitedly, "but don't you think it's been the best part so far, the least scary part? We've had to walk a lot, but there haven't been any horrible creatures, or anything chasing us. No dragons. And now we can fly on these marvellous birds, which will probably take us exactly where we want to go, because that's what happens in a computer game, isn't it? The things – birds in this case – that you find to help you, they're pre-programmed to do the right thing, the same as the things that hinder you are programmed to do what they do. That's right, isn't it? So the birds will take us to the valley."

Chris nodded slowly. Everything Amy had said was absolutely right. He didn't know why he hadn't thought of it that way himself. He had played enough computer games in his time.

And yet to climb on the back of a huge bird was undeniably one of the strangest things he had ever done, or even imagined doing. He watched Amy and the Little Princess do it first. Each settled on the back of an uncomplaining bird, Amy smiling from ear to ear and exclaiming over how cushiony and cosy the plumage felt. The Little Princess needed a hand up, but she was soon sitting silently, her fingers twined in the feathers, her face relaxed, as if this was how she always travelled.

Chris had to nerve himself to climb onto the remaining Raja Bird – he was worried that taking a grip on its feathers might hurt the creature and upset it. But it seemed quite unperturbed and Amy was right – sitting in the plumage *was* like sinking into a deep, soft bedcover. The slight spread of the bird's wings allowed him to reach out and take a grip on the edge of the long wing-bone.

In front of him, Amy's bird took a couple of quick steps and launched itself into the air, closely followed by the bird on which the Little Princess sat. Within seconds, Chris was airborne, too. He couldn't help gasping at the sudden movement of the wings and the swiftness of the bird's rise into the air. He gripped tightly as it wheeled in a half circle, following the other two birds, then flew straight ahead, high above the plain they had looked out over just a few minutes before.

Amy's delighted laughter floated back to him and Chris was glad to hear it. He thought it had a silvery sound, a lightness to it, like bubbles. He smiled and let his body relax. There was only one thing to do when flying high in the sky on a great bird's back. Enjoy it.

Since being plunged inside the game, Chris and Amy had known terror and triumph, disappointment and delight, felt the drag of exhaustion and the surge of excitement. Some of it, Chris thought, might be forgotten in time, but not this. Not riding high on this great bird, whose powerful wings cut the air with an audible swoosh as it banked or climbed, or rode the sky in silence, gliding huge distances at a stretch. He would never, never forget this.

Perhaps if he tried hang-gliding one day, it could be as breathtaking as this, but there wouldn't be soft plumage and a living body beneath him. There wouldn't be the sight of the great head in front of him, the sun flashing on the curve of its beak. Once, as the bird turned its head, Chris saw the shine in its eye, glowing like an ember.

Looking down on the shadows cast by the carrier birds, he exulted yet again at not having to walk the long track below them.

Eventually, the birds' shadows were joined by those cast by the rock tors that now dotted the plain. The track wound on and on below them as the tors became larger and more numerous and the landscape changed into rocky hills. The hills were covered in foliage of an unusual purple-green shade. The birds flew lower.

There was a sudden squeal ahead, from either Amy or the Little Princess, but, when he checked, the two were still sitting securely on their birds. Chris looked down and saw an appalling sight. Intermittently, long, thin arms, coloured the same unusual purple-green as the forest, groped upwards, surmounted by hands that looked as if they meant to snatch whatever was above them. Chris couldn't make out whether the arms were actually attached to the trees – part of them – or whether they belonged to some weird creatures living in the trees.

Wings swished on either side of him as the three birds rose higher. Had they simply been showing their passengers what they would have had to walk through? Chris shuddered and felt a wave of gratitude that they weren't on foot down there.

Now the mountain forest became a more familiar green beneath him and Chris took a tighter grip on the feathers. He was afraid he might forget to hang on if he didn't concentrate, because a very exciting idea had just struck him.

If the birds had flown them over the horrific Forest of Groping Hands, why could they not fly them over the valley of the Mountain Beast? Were they going to do it anyway, without any prompting? Were they heading straight for the princess's kingdom? She had said the Raja Birds sometimes went there. Was this glorious ride going to end in a glorious victory – the return of the Little Princess direct to her kingdom and its people? If so, there would be no need for a confrontation with the Mountain Beast.

Even as he allowed himself the indulgence of such thoughts, Chris's bird, following the other two, caught a down draught and glided towards the ground. Down, down, down.

Chris's thoughts whirled. They were still in mountain country. This was not the princess's kingdom. He must try to encourage the Raja Birds up again. He must try to persuade them to fly on.

"Up!" he cried. "Up! On to the kingdom of the Little Princess. Up! Up!"

It was no use. The birds landed in an open circle of land almost ringed by forest, except for a wooded valley that Chris recognised with a sinking heart. It was the valley of the Mountain Beast.

Amy and the Little Princes slid off their birds and Amy stood beside hers, stroking the coffee-brown feathers of its breast. "If you were mine forever, I would call you Mocha," she said. "Thank you. Thank you so much for our wonderful ride!"

Chris climbed off his bird. He had to face that it was as Amy had so correctly predicted when she talked about the programming of the game. When players realised they could ride the birds, they were only able to fly to this spot. He and Amy were players who could alter their destiny within the confines of the game by the choices they made. But only the players could choose and, no matter what the players wished, the birds could not respond.

The two cousins and the princess stood watching as the Raja Birds stretched their necks and then their wings.

"They're like runners flexing their muscles before they run!" exclaimed Amy in delight. Then, sure enough, the birds ran a few short steps and winged their way back up into the sky. As he watched them circle twice above them and then fly back the way they had come, Chris marvelled at Amy's observation and understanding of animal behaviour.

He took a seat next to her on a fallen log. They both felt some need to pause between flying and walking. "Don't ask us to hurry, will you?" Amy said to the Little Princess. "We'll be moving on very soon."

She turned to Chris. "First, I want to think about how wonderful that was – just for a minute or two. I'll never forget it!"

"I won't either," agreed Chris. It would have been even better still if the Raja Birds had flown them on to the princess's kingdom, but he found he was able to accept the fact that they couldn't. Maybe his spirits had been permanently lifted by the thrilling ride. "I've never done anything so amazing. I'd have expected to get cold way up there. I wonder why we didn't?"

"Maybe it was the cushiony feathers. We were at least half protected by them. Wasn't it incredible!"

"Was it you who squealed?"

"No, it was the princess. It made me look down though. What about those revolting hands and arms!" Amy shivered. The scary memory seemed to remind her of where they were now. "Is that the valley?" she asked. "Is that the valley of the Mountain Beast?"

Chris nodded. "We can move closer before we meet the beast, I think. We could look at the sides and see how steep they are."

"Come on then. Let's do it."

As they got to their feet, the Little Princess turned with what looked like eagerness towards the valley and the road forward.

Chris nudged Amy. "She knows she's nearly home."

"And we have to make sure that she gets there." There was determination in Amy's voice and Chris knew, as they moved across the clearing and into the valley, that she was searching her mind for a strategy, a way to divert the creature so that Chris and the Little Princess could skirt by it unnoticed.

Chris knew he would have to calculate the length of the beast's chain, so he could figure out how high they would need to go to be out of its reach. He was already scanning the sides of the valley and observing the terrain. It was rocky and rugged, with a lot of thick undergrowth beneath large trees. The undergrowth would make good cover.

"Shouldn't you and the Little Princess be hiding back here, so that the Mountain Beast doesn't know you're here?" asked Amy. "Then it won't be watching for you when I try the diversion."

"I don't know," pondered Chris. "What sort of diversion are you thinking of?"

"I wish I had something that would make a lot of noise, like a drum or something else I could hit with a stick."

"We have the stick," said Chris.

"But nothing to bang it on," replied Amy.

"We should all stay together," said the Little Princess suddenly. Since entering the valley, her behaviour had changed. Now, instead of walking alongside Chris, she stayed just behind him, as if he were her shield against danger.

"We will for a little bit," Chris assured her before turning to Amy. "I don't think it'll make any difference if the beast sees us all. You need to see it and know what it looks like before we try and work out together the best way to divert it. I think it could be just around the bend actually."

Chris tightened his grip on the stick. It was a feeble weapon, but at least it was something to hold onto. He was filled with a sudden desire to turn back. Surely it was better to face any of the dangers they had come through rather than the Mountain Beast, pacing up and down across the one path to the kingdom of the Little Princess?

"After we've got past the beast, we've done it, haven't we? I mean, we'll be able to deliver the princess safe and sound? And we'll be able to go home?" There was an edge of longing in Amy's words.

"Yes," said Chris quietly, "we'll be able to go home." He wondered how that was ever going to happen.

WHOLE AND FREE

They heard the Mountain Beast before they saw it – the clanking of its chain as it paced the narrow path at the bottom of the valley and its call – an odd, moaning sound that was neither a cry nor a roar. Then, suddenly, there it was.

Amy clutched Chris's free hand as she walked beside him and he heard her gasp and swallow.

"Is that it?" Her voice was a whisper as she stared at the animal that had appeared ahead of them. "It's . . . it's *really* scary! And really huge!"

Chris nodded. For a moment neither of them spoke, then Chris said, "We'll keep going forward. You need to get an idea of how close you can go and still be safe. Then we'll go back a little and work out a plan."

The beast became rapidly larger and larger as they advanced. It was as though the computer zoom command was bringing it closer. Chris could hear Amy muttering beside him, "I have to be brave. I have to be brave . . ." and he realised she wasn't aware she was speaking aloud.

The creature stood far taller than all of them on four long, strong limbs. The lower parts of its legs and feet were covered in green scales, and the upper legs and body were covered in hair. From the mass of tangled, black hair rose its head, also covered in green scales and shaped like that of an enormous cat. Two short, twisted horns thrust out from behind the ears, and the eyes were like human eyes but much larger. They glinted with anger and Chris shuddered at the sight of them.

The beast's cavernous mouth was ringed with sharp teeth, and sharp, silver claws curled from its feet, but it was the eyes that truly frightened Chris.

"Stay here, Amy," he said, knowing that the Little Princess would stay back with her. "I'll move up just a little bit more. And that will be about as far as any of us should go."

He had to make himself go closer. It would help Amy to feel brave if he showed some bravery himself. As long as he looked brave on the outside, she would never know how he really felt inside. The frantic beating of his heart filled his entire body. He needed to take control. Fear could easily slide into panic and panic would make him helpless. Worst of all, it might infect Amy.

He felt Amy let go his hand and became aware that the Little Princess was clutching at the leg of his jeans. "Stay with Amy," he hissed, realising once more that they were all dependent on what he did next.

The beast had looked fearsome on the computer screen, but, standing here in front of it, smelling its smell, seeing the shine of its scales and the hairs of its coat, hearing its heavy breathing, he was truly horrified. The Mountain Beast stared back at him. Then its eyes flashed and it turned towards the mountains and opened its mouth to let out a long, wild call. Was it some sort of challenge?

Chris had managed to push down his fear – just a little – but the effort seemed wasted as the fear rose again, snaking up through his rib cage and gripping his heart. His hands trembled as they clutched the stick. A stick! What an apology of a weapon to use against this creature! Chris wished he had the power to turn the puny stick into a mighty sword.

"Stay near," Chris called to the Little Princess. "You're safe there. I'm just taking one step more and you'll see, Amy, that you shouldn't go any closer than that." He hoped his voice sounded brave, that they couldn't hear it tremble, like his hands on the stick.

He took another step. Then the Little Princess's scream mingled with his howl of horror as he realised he had misjudged the reach of the Mountain Beast. One quick paw darted forward, a silver claw hooked into his clothing and he was flicked through the air like a flimsy plaything.

His shriek gradually died away as he found himself lying beneath the Mountain Beast's hairy body, surrounded by four scaly legs. What should he do next? What *could* he do? Was there a chance to do anything in this ghastly predicament, or would he be scooped straight into the mighty mouth of the beast?

Panic churned in Chris's mind; his legs and arms turned as limp as rags. Inside his chest, his heartbeat pounded like a drum.

Then, unexpectedly, he felt his voice rising in his throat. He could still speak. "Help me, Amy!" he managed hoarsely. His voice gathered strength. "Help me!" he shrieked.

He hadn't realised that the Little Princess would think that he was calling for *her* help. Nor could he see her stretch out a trembling hand and toss the jewel into the air, once, twice, then a third time. But he heard a tearing sound and turned his head away from the fearsome brightness as lightning slashed close to him.

He caught the awful smell of burning skin and singed hair and knew that lightning had struck the Mountain Beast. He heard agonised cries and, instead of a hairy belly above him, he saw the sky as the beast suddenly tipped sideways and collapsed.

Chris leapt to his feet and stared down at the fallen monster. Amy was close by, and beside her was the Little Princess, thrusting the stick into his hands.

"Kill him! Now!" she ordered.

Relief at his escape from what seemed a certain and terrible death flooded through Chris as he took the stick from the princess and stepped back a pace or two, his eyes on the crippled Mountain Beast. Its wounds were terrible. It took each breath with a shallow gasp, and let it out with a low whimper.

All Chris had to do was raise the stick – the puny stick that could, after all, be useful – and bring it down on the creature's helpless head. It was what he would have done, with the click of a mouse button, if he were sitting at the computer playing this game. He grasped the stick more tightly and began to lift it.

Suddenly, there was a hand on his arm. "Oh, Chris." It was Amy's voice. "You can't kill him. Look at his eyes!"

Chris stared into the Mountain Beast's eyes. They weren't glinting with anger as they had before. Unbelievably, they were now filled with pleading. Chris wished yet again that he wasn't inside the game but outside, looking at this creature on the screen, where he could feel quite detached from it. Here, in its presence, an entirely different set of emotions were awakened and became entwined in the game. He could see and smell burnt flesh. He could hear the low moans and whimpers. And his gaze was locked onto the begging eyes of a dreadfully wounded creature.

Amy was only a step or two away from the creature's face. "His eyes aren't fierce now, Chris. They're trying to talk to us. He's trying to tell us he's hurt – badly."

"Kill him!" The Little Princess's voice had risen to a pitch they had never heard before. She was so close to her kingdom and this beast was the last thing that could prevent her from getting there.

Chris wanted to believe that Amy, the animal lover, was wrong, that she was giving way to emotion and imagining the feelings of this monster before him. Even more, he wanted to believe that the princess's demand was fair and reasonable.

But he couldn't. The longer he gazed into the eyes of the Mountain Beast, the more he realised that Amy was right. The creature was trying to talk with its eyes. Its plea for help was clear.

The last vestiges of fear were washed away by a wave of sympathy. He imagined how this animal must feel, chained in this narrow valley when the mountains were its home. He imagined, too, how it must feel to fight endless battles instead of roaming free.

Crouched beside the beast, Amy reached out to stroke the coarse hair above the scales. "He's badly hurt, Chris. He can't stop us getting past now, even if he wants to. We can't kill him! We should help him!"

It was true. The Mountain Beast was incapable of stopping them in its present state. The Little Princess could pass on to her kingdom with nothing to fear. Chris reached up to the thick leather collar around the Mountain Beast's neck and managed to undo the buckle and drag it away. The beast's breathing did not ease, but its eyes grew steadier, less panic-stricken.

"Kill him! Kill him!" cried the Little Princess.

Her fearful cry brought Chris's gaze back to the dangerous claws gleaming so close – yet he could see the calmness in the Mountain Beast's eyes. He thought of the cavernous mouth filled with teeth – yet the burn wounds were more terrible.

Then he remembered what was in his pocket. "Go! Go on ahead, it's safe now!" Chris called to the princess. "I'll catch up with you."

He lifted the head of the Mountain Beast and, as much as he was able, propped it on his shoulder. Then he pulled the Health Vial from his pocket and unscrewed the metal lid. Reaching as far as he could past the gaping jaws and lolling tongue, he poured the contents of the vial down the beast's throat. For a moment or two, he held its scaly head, then laid it back on the ground. It was the only help he could offer and he had no idea if it would be of any use at all.

Tears were trickling down Amy's face, though she tried to smile. "Will it help, do you think?"

"I don't know," said Chris with a weary shrug. "I don't know."

He glanced ahead to where the princess was stumbling along the rocky path and he knew they should hurry after her, but now something truly astounding was happening.

Chris and Amy drew back as the Mountain Beast rose to its feet. The wounds opened by the lightning were closing over. New black hair was springing into place on the singed and raw flesh. Without its heavy, dragging chain, the monster's head rose proudly on its shoulders. The Health Vial had performed a miracle.

Suddenly, the beast gave another long, wild cry. The hairs stood up on Chris's neck and he stood frozen for an instant as fear returned in a paralysing wave. But the creature only bent its head, and touched Chris's nose with his own. It was like a kiss and, as the warm breath of the Mountain Beast mixed with his own shallow panting, Chris's fear was gone as quickly as it came. Stiffly, the great beast moved on towards Amy and touched her nose as it had Chris's.

For a moment or two longer, Chris and Amy stood watching as the huge creature, whole and free, wheeled about and loped off to its mountain home.

SOMETHING SOLID UNDERNEATH

Amy watched the Mountain Beast return home through tears that ran down her face unchecked. Chris knew that they were tears of joy as well as relief that the last task was over. Who would not feel joy for an animal released from torment? He felt it, but it was time to go.

"Amy, we have to catch up with the princess."

"I know." Amy smiled through her tears. "I don't want to miss her homecoming. I'm trying to imagine what her people will be like? Do you think they'll be as tiny as she is?"

"Only one way to find out. Come on."

The Little Princess had gone beyond the point where the pathway curved around a bend and left the valley. Amy and Chris ran to catch up, their hearts singing. There was nothing left to fear.

Around the corner they came to an abrupt stop.

Ahead of them, the Little Princess had picked up her skirts and was wading through the shallow waters of an enormous, silver lake. On its distant shore rose the spires of what must be her castle. She was not letting even a vast lake prevent her from heading for home.

Chris ran forward and splashed into the water behind her. "What are you doing?" he called.

"Wait! Wait! Be careful!" shouted Amy.

The Little Princess's tinkling laugh reached them from over her shoulder. "It's only to my knees. You may follow me to . . ."

Suddenly, she began to sink, her skirts puffing up around her on the glimmering water. "Help! Help!" she called, her little limbs thrashing so that she rose again briefly, and then sank once more.

Chris was the champion swimmer but it was Amy who leapt past him in a shallow dive. She grabbed at the Little Princess, who continued to rise and sink as she struggled and gulped and squealed.

Amy was standing beside her now, and the water didn't even reach her shoulders. "It's all right! Stay still! Stay still! I've got you."

The silver lake no longer looked as harmless as it had just seconds ago. A wind was whipping the surface into curling wavelets. They splashed up and into the face of the Little Princess, even though Amy tried to hold her above the water level.

Chris came alongside. "Give her to me. I'm a bit taller than you."

Amy helped the Little Princess climb onto Chris's back.

"I never managed to pass the Mountain Beast when I played the game on the computer," Chris told Amy, "so I didn't know this lake was here. Now I'm not sure what to do next."

"It's not as if you've never had *that* feeling before," remarked Amy wryly. "But only the princess is out of her depth, because she's so tiny. *We're* not."

"No kidding?" muttered Chris, peeved by Amy's summation of the obvious. "But further out we may find ourselves out of our depth, too. We don't know, do we? Are you confident in deep water?"

Now it was Amy's turn to be indignant. "Of course. If I'm swimming on my own, that is. It's not so far to go."

"You must get me to the castle," said the princess. A tear was tracing a shiny path down her exquisite little face. "Don't you see that I am nearly home?" Though her voice remained as impassive as ever, she clung to Chris like a limpet and repeatedly scanned the water surrounding them.

"What we need is a boat, or even a log," said Chris. "I could put the Little Princess in it, or on it, and swim on my back towing it. I wonder if there's something back –"

A splashing sound came from somewhere behind them and a large swell lifted and dropped them as it rolled by. Was the storm getting worse?

"Are you all right, Amy?" Chris called. For a moment, he couldn't see her as the next wave rolled between them.

Chris concentrated on keeping the Little Princess's head above water. They were so close! The castle with its glinting towers was right there – across the lake. Surely, on the brink of success and after all they had gone through, they couldn't fail now?

All at once, Chris felt something rising beneath him – something solid that was lifting him and the Little Princess above the churning water. A fearful, mad thought flashed through his head. Didn't volcanoes sometimes rise suddenly out of water?

"I'm here," cried Amy's voice behind him. "What's happening?"

One arm still around the Little Princess, Chris flailed about him for support with the other – and found his fingers meeting and twining into something that felt very much like hair.

It *was* hair! Just ahead of them, the green, horned head of the Mountain Beast had risen above the waves. The solid shape that had lifted them above the water was his great back. It seemed unbelievable, but it was true.

"Amy! It's helping us! The Mountain Beast has come to help us!" Surprised, delighted and exhausted, Chris began to laugh, and soon Amy joined him.

Almost hysterical with relief and joy, they rode across the lake, high above the rolling waves, saved by the creature they had most feared. When they reached the shallows on the other side, underneath the gold-tipped spires of the stone castle, the Mountain Beast stopped swimming to let them slide off its body. Then, without pausing, it turned and swam back the way it had come, creating a huge wake in the silver water behind it.

Suddenly, the Little Princess, who had ridden across the lake with unruffled confidence, was squealing again. Chris held her hand as the waters rocked about them and then finally began to still. In the distance, the Mountain Beast's wake grew smaller and smaller as it headed towards the mountains of home.

"Aren't you glad we didn't kill him?" Amy whispered.

"Really glad," said Chris quietly. "Really glad." He brushed away a few stray tears trickling down his face. He didn't know if they were tears of gladness or sadness – maybe they were tears of exhaustion. But he did know he was never likely to see the Mountain Beast again.

The Little Princess hadn't waited to bid farewell to the great creature she had feared so much. While Chris and Amy watched the beast swim away, she took her hand from Chris's and began to wade through the last few metres of shallow water, her gaze fixed firmly on the shores of her kingdom.

Amy turned to watch her. "Look! Look what she's doing!"

With both tiny feet at last on dry land, the princess had paused to throw the jewel into the air, displaying her proof that she was no impostor. And, as the lightning flashed in a banner of celebration above them, her subjects gathered to welcome their princess home.

The people who came running to swell the crowd below the castle were all as small as the Little Princess herself. "It's sort of like staring at a fantasy movie," murmured Amy as she and Chris stood in the shallows, watching. "But they're real people and we're actually here." She shook her head and drops of water flicked outwards. "It's all so unbelievable."

"Look," said Chris suddenly. "She's beckoning to us. She wants us to come." He turned to Amy. "We've finished though, haven't we? We've completed the Seven Missions. She doesn't need us now."

Amy nodded in agreement. "I'd like to see inside the castle. But you're right, the Little Princess doesn't need us any more." A frown appeared on her face. "How will we get back across the lake? How will we get home?"

Chris was only half listening. He waved to the Little Princess, then half turned away from her, still waving, trying to show her they wouldn't be joining her.

The Little Princess lowered her beckoning hand and fumbled in the folds of her gown. She raised her hand high again and Chris thought she was waving back to him. Instead, she threw something that arced upwards and down, glowing like a fire coal as it whistled through the air. Chris reached out to catch it.

"It's the jewel!" he cried. "It's her jewel!"

Now they saw that the Little Princess *was* waving to them, but only for a moment before she turned her back. The crowd parted to allow her through, then followed as she walked towards the castle doors.

Chris stared down at the jewel sparkling on his open palm. "Why have we got it? Why did she throw it and go?"

Amy knew why. "It's her gift. It's her gift to you for saving her."

Astonished, Chris turned the glittering gem over in his hand. "I can't believe it would be a gift for me. She didn't ever say thank you, did she?"

"Well, she's rolled every thank you she should have said into one gift," said Amy. "I guess she doesn't need the jewel any more."

"You helped save her, too."

"I only helped by default – because I was there. It was you who cared enough to *want* to save her."

"Well, the jewel should be for both of us, not just for me."

Amy shrugged and then grinned. "You're the computer freak. You're the –"

She stopped mid-sentence and stared, open-mouthed, around her. There was no castle, no lake, no princess. There was just a desk in front of them and a computer screen that had been turned off . . .

"We're back!" cried Chris. "Game over! We've come back!"

A strange feeling came over him. It was like waking suddenly from a dream, but it had been no dream. He had been in deserts and tunnels, over chasms and up a tower. He had escaped from rampaging guards and wild creatures. He had rescued Amy from a dragon and she had rescued him from a ravine.

He had run and walked and climbed. He had flown on the back of a bird. He had feared and then cared for a monstrous creature. He had crossed a lake on that beast's back. He had saved a princess. All this, and here he was sitting at a desk as if none of it had ever happened.

Amy's voice broke into his confusion. "We're still wet, Chris. Look – my clothes are dripping on the floor! So are yours! It all happened. It really did happen!"

There was the sound of a door opening behind them. "Oh, there you are." It was Chris's mother.

"We've been looking for you." Auntie May's voice sounded mildly cross.

Chris and Amy stared at the adults coming through the doorway and then back at each other. How would they ever be able to explain their absence when *they* couldn't understand it?

"Where have you been?" asked Auntie May. "We thought you were here playing a computer game."

"And then you weren't here when we came looking for you," added Chris's mother.

"We *were* playing a game," began Amy, "and then . . . somehow we were . . ."

Hastily, Chris interrupted. It was no good trying to explain until they had thought it all through and at least begun to find a thread of logic behind it all. "She means it was so exciting that we had to leave it and go outside for a bit."

"In the rain?" asked his mother, her tone disbelieving.

Chris and Amy both glanced out the window. It hadn't been raining earlier on.

Chris's mother came closer. "You're soaking wet! Both of you. That was a bit silly, Chris, taking your cousin outside in the rain."

"It was my fault really," said Amy.

As she spoke, Chris watched her eyes following the cable that led across the room from the computer and through the hole in the screen. Could the whole thing have been caused by something so simple? A single cable?

"Oh well, no harm done," said Auntie May. "A bit

of rain won't hurt you, I guess. Come on upstairs now and we'll all have some afternoon tea. I've learned how to make the most amazing chocolate cake – you'll love it.

"I did turn off that computer before, didn't I?" she added, giving Chris and Amy a bright smile. "We thought you'd finished your game, you see. It said on the screen, *Seven Missions completed. The Little Princess has been returned to her kingdom. Well done.*"

"Did it?" asked Chris eagerly. "Did it say that before you turned the computer off?"

"Yes," said Auntie May. "It did."

"And I turned off that switch behind the screen," said Chris's mother, frowning a little. "You know, Auntie May did ask you not to touch things in there."

"Well, I didn't say that *exactly*, though I guess it was what I meant. I should have made it clearer." May gave another bright smile. "No harm done. Off we go then."

"You've managed to get awfully scruffy, Chris," his mother said behind him as they went up the stairs. "In fact, the pair of you look as if you've been playing some sort of wild game, not sitting in front of a computer screen."

Amy opened her mouth to speak, but Chris shot her a look and she stayed silent.

Later that evening, Chris explained to Amy how he felt. "I think we should think everything through ourselves before we try to tell anyone else what happened."

"Well I can't *stop* thinking about it," said Amy. "When you have a dream, it stays for a while and then it disappears and you know it was just a dream. But I know that what we've just done *wasn't* a dream. For one thing, I'm so tired. I feel as if I've run the cross-country as a sprint! I could go to bed right this minute and fall asleep before I pulled the blanket over me."

"I feel a bit the same," said Chris, "but I need to talk, too. If I knew why it all happened, I think I could enjoy looking back on it. Riding on that Raja Bird! I'll never forget it!"

"And we'll never forget the Mountain Beast you were so scared of –"

"So were you."

"I certainly was! We'll certainly never forget it turning into something almost human."

Chris knew she was right. They *would* never forget, but right now he was tussling with other memories. "I'm remembering other things, too – things I've read about new computer technology developments that would blow your brain."

"Such as?" asked Amy.

"Well, one thing I read recently was that in one country – Japan I think – they say they'll soon have computers that can show, on-screen, what's on your mind. I can't quite make enough of a leap to really understand that as a concept."

"I'm not surprised," murmured Amy.

"I'm trying to work out if something like that happened with us."

"That's crazy, Chris. I would never have imagined even half the things that happened to us, so they weren't in my mind before appearing on-screen. Anyway, what happened to us was the other way round. It wasn't happening on a screen. That was the trouble! We were *inside* the game!"

Chris shook his head as if to clear it. "You're right, of course. It's just that there are amazing things happening in the world of technology and maybe – just maybe – Uncle Reg was up there. Maybe he was a super genius, quietly working in his own little corner and inventing amazing things that he hadn't got around to telling the world about."

"I do still wonder if it was something to do with that connecting cord. Perhaps he'd found some way to travel into a game? So you wouldn't just be there in a virtual way, but *really* be there. The thing I can't work out is, how can you travel into something that isn't really real to begin with?"

"Well, I don't think there's any way we could possibly have *imagined* it was real. And that's what people will say if we tell them about it. How could two of us imagine exactly the same thing at the same time?"

"And be . . . well, sort of united in the happenings while we imagined it all." Amy made a despairing face. "Let's not try to think any more tonight."

"Okay," said Chris.

They sat for a while on the garden chairs, each thinking their own thoughts. Then Chris drew the princess's jewel out of his pocket and placed it on the table beside them.

"If we had imagined it, we wouldn't have this."

For a long moment, they both stared at the glow of the Little Princess's jewel, while a tumble of memories cascaded through their minds.

"Could you try . . ." began Amy, but her question died away as she stared at the jewel.

Chris picked it up and looked straight at Amy. "Could I try throwing it in the air three times? Is that what you were going to say?"

Amy nodded.

"But I won't have the power or the connection with the jewel that the Little Princess had, will I?"

"I think maybe, when she gave you the jewel, she passed the power on to you."

Chris stared at Amy and then back at the stone. It was a beautiful evening, clear and still now after the earlier rain. Chris's father had said that, when he came in from the garden for dinner, he could smell the edge of spring in the air.

"Follow me," said Chris, getting to his feet.

Chris led Amy to the bottom of the garden and they stood behind the hedge that screened the vegetable garden from the lawn.

"Okay, here goes." Chris held the jewel out in front of him, resting on his hand. It was a beautiful thing. He paused. "Just remember that I'm only doing this once. Ever."

His heart began beating faster as he threw the jewel three times into the air.

Up-FLASH-down-catch, up-FLASH-down-catch, up-FLASH-down-catch.

He and Amy just had time to draw in a breath

before lightning tore through the sky in a yellow, zigzag ribbon. It was as bright as the lightning that had flashed when the princess had tossed the jewel.

"It's the proof, isn't it?" breathed Amy, her eyes still fixed on the sky.

"For us," agreed Chris. "Proof for us that we were there, but to prove to anyone else that we were really inside the game, we'd have to do it again. We'd have to get inside a game again – if we could work out exactly how – and take someone else with us."

Another voice interrupted. It was Chris's mother calling them from the back door. "Come on in, you two. We don't want you getting wet twice in one day."

Chris rolled his eyes at Amy. "As if getting wet is the only thing that's happened to us today."

"It's not raining, you know," said Chris when they reached the doorstep and saw the adults gathered by the door, waiting for them.

"Not yet, but it will," said Chris's father. "Didn't you see that lightning?"